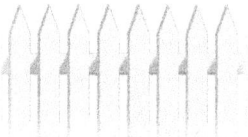

The Tug of Home
Restful Words for Weary Families

The Tug of Home
Restful Words for Weary Families

Charles E. Poole

ISBN 1-57312-704-2

The Tug of Home
Restful Words for Weary Families

Charles E. Poole

Copyright © 1997
Peake Road

6316 Peake Road
Macon, Georgia 31210-3960
1-800-747-3016

Peake Road is an imprint of
Smyth and Helwys Publishing Inc.

All rights reserved.
Printed in the United States of America.

Biblical quotations, unless otherwise noted, are
from the New Revised Standard Version of the Bible (NRSV).

Library of Congress Cataloging-in-Publication Data

Poole, Charles E.
    The tug of home: restful words for weary families/
    Charles E. Poole.
    viii + 120pp.   6" x 9" (15 x 23 cm.)
    ISBN 1-57312-704-2
    1. Family—Religious life.
    2. Families—Prayer books and devotionals—English.
    I. Title.
    BV4526.2.P56   1997
    249—dc21   97-6828
                                                                         CIP

*Dedicated to Joshua and Maria,
gifts of God's grace to Marcia and me*

Contents

Introduction: A Log-Brief-Tearful-Joyful-Dash	1
Will Someone Say the Blessing?	5
When a Family Moves	21
Letting Go and Going On	33
You Are Here	41
When Is Enough Enough?	51
What Will the Children Remember?	59
When a Family Faces Death	65
Life, In the Light of Death	71
When Families Say Goodbye	79
Who You Are Is Who You Were	83
Who's That on Your Refrigerator?	89
How Does Christmas Feel?	93
So Take a Lot of Pictures	99
The Tug of Home	103
Epilogue: The Picture Spills Over the Frame	113

Introduction

A Long-Brief-Tearful-Joyful-Dash

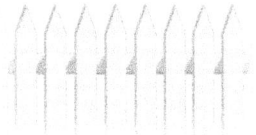

President Jimmy Carter, in his beautiful and powerful book, *Living Faith*, tells about one of the most unforgettable sermons he has ever heard. It was preached by a minister named Otis Moss at the funeral service for Mrs. Martin Luther King, Sr. The unforgettable sermon was all about what the Reverend Mr. Moss called "the little dash in between." President Carter recalls that the preacher said there would be a marker on Mrs. King's grave with her name and a couple of dates, the date when she was born and the date when she died, and a little dash in between the two dates. The preacher then said that he didn't want to talk about the date when Mrs. King was born, or the date when she died, but about "that little dash" between those two dates.[1]

Our life, the part that comes between the day we were born and the day we will die, is, indeed, a dash. It is a long dash, full of growing and changing. But it is also a brief dash, always fleeting and passing. It is a sometimes tearful dash, bruised by heartbreak and pain. But it is a frequently joyful dash, colored by the happiness and love of faith, family, friendship, and home.

The words that have found a home inside the walls of this book hope to give a little help to families who are weary from the pace and the strain of the dash. After all, families these days could use a little help. Families have always needed a little help, but, these days, families seem to need a little help even more than ever before. Families are weary from overburdened schedules. Families are fragmented by overcommitted calendars. Families are moving from place to place, which means families are saying some painful goodbyes to some beloved places and some dear people. Families need a little help, help to hold on and let go, help to say hello and goodbye to new friends and old places, help to live through the changes and struggles that every family will eventually have to face.

The words that have found a home in the shade of this book are traveling around in theological reflections and devotional essays that hope to offer families a little help. These reflections and essays hope to help families think about life's most ordinary moments and most difficult struggles in the light of the grace of God that has been revealed to us in the life of our Lord Jesus. The long-brief-tearful-joyful-dash that marks the place between birth and death is filled with laughter and tears, with hellos and goodbyes, with joy and pain, with holding on and letting go. These theological reflections and devotional essays hope to help, not in the final resolution of those family ambiguities, but in the naming and facing and living of them.

Charles E. Poole
Washington, D.C.
Lent, 1997

Will Someone Say the Blessing?

If they ever hold a contest for "The World's Saddest Sentence," I think I know one that should be among the five finalists. The sad sentence that gets my vote is Esau's plea for his father's blessing. Seldom has there been a sadder sentence said than Esau's poignant cry, "Have you only one blessing, Father? Bless me, me also, Father."

Esau cried, "Bless me, too, Daddy, bless me too," and, ever since, his sad sentence has never lacked for an echo. Esau's quivering lips trembled those words into the air, and, though it has since been a long time, those words have never yet fallen to the ground. Esau's voice has found its echo in every generation. Nobody wants to live an unblessed life. Everybody yearns to hear someone say the blessing to them, for them, and about them.

The intriguing events that preceded Esau's sad sentence constitute one of the most familiar, and fascinating, stories in the whole Bible. It is a story that could well serve as a laboratory for marriage and family therapists, because it is crowded with such family issues as sibling rivalry, parents identifying more with one child than another, children and parents forming alliances that subsequently pit mother and father against one another, and disputes over who gets what when the estate is settled. It's all there, tucked away in the intriguing saga of Isaac and Rebekah and their adult sons, Jacob and Esau.

The emotional hinge on which the story turns is this whole matter of "the blessing." As the scene unfolds in Genesis 27, the aged father, Isaac, calls in his older son, Esau, and says, "My son, I am old, and I could die any day. So I want you to go out and hunt a deer and prepare it for me. Then, we will eat the venison, and I will give you the blessing before I die." So far, the scene is simple. But the plot soon thickens. Trouble looms on the horizon.

Rebekah, Isaac's wife, was in the next room and overheard this conversation between her husband and her son. Now, she wanted Jacob to receive the blessing instead of Esau. (No one should be surprised by this little bend in the story. After all, way back in Genesis 25:27-28, the writer dropped at our feet a flirtatious little handkerchief embroidered with this faint hint of trouble to come:

> When the boys grew up, Esau was a skillful hunter, a man of the field, while Jacob was a quiet man, living in tents. Isaac loved Esau, because he was fond of game; but Rebekah loved Jacob.

With those words, the writer was warning us of trouble to come!)

So, Rebekah went to work on a plan to deceive her nearly-blind husband into blessing Jacob instead of Esau. While Esau was out hunting for Isaac's deer, Rebekah was busy cooking a goat, sprinkling it liberally with a local culinary additive known as "Aunt Lerr's Bouquet," a venison-flavored gravy mix reputed to make a goat taste dear to even the most discriminating palate. But, when she had the meal ready and called Jacob to take it in to his father, he got cold feet. Jacob feared that, even if the goat did taste like the venison Isaac had requested, Isaac might reach out and touch Jacob, and thus discover that the bearer of the meal was not his hairy son Esau, but his smooth son Jacob. But, not to worry. Rebekah thinks of everything:

> "Take it [this food] to your father to eat, so that he may bless you before he dies." But Jacob said to his mother Rebekah, "Look, my brother Esau is a hairy man, and I am a man of smooth skin. Perhaps my father will feel me." . . . Then Rebekah took the best garments of her elder son Esau . . . and put them on her son Jacob; and she put the skins of the kids on his hands and on the smooth part of his neck. Then she handed the savory food, and the bread that she had prepared, to her son Jacob. (27:10-11, 15-17)

That Rebekah . . . she was pretty tricky. She had dressed her son to trick his father and cheat his brother. And it worked. With his hands disguised in goat hair and the entree incognito in imitation deer gravy, Jacob approached his aged father and said, "I am Esau. I did like you said and fixed you venison. Now sit up and eat it so you can bless me." Well, at this point, the ruse almost broke down, because Isaac said, "How did you go hunting, find a deer, and barbecue it so quickly?" Jacob, always nimble on his feet, said, "Well, uh, the Lord just blessed me with quick success." Then Isaac said, "Are you sure you are Esau? Your voice sounds like Jacob." Jacob said, "Of course, I'm Esau. Feel my hairy arms. Smell my hunting jacket." Finally, blind old Isaac said, "Well, you do feel like Esau, and you do smell like Esau, so you must be Esau." And with that, Isaac ate the meal and gave his blessing to the son who he thought was Esau, but who, of course, was actually Jacob.

Having secured his father's blessing, Jacob left. No sooner had he gone out than Esau came in with the real meal from the real deer that he had hunted and prepared for his father. He said, "Okay, Dad. Here's the meal you requested. I fixed it the way you like it. You ready to eat?" And, in that moment, blind old Isaac knew that he had been had, tricked, deceived, and duped. He said to Esau, "Son, I'm sorry. I've already given the blessing to your brother. I thought he was you, and I blessed him."

Now, right about here, you and I are thinking, "Well, this is simple to fix. Just call that rascal Jacob back in, tell him his little charade has been uncovered, take back the blessing, and give it to Esau." But that is not possible. In the world of Isaac and Rebekah, Jacob and Esau, once a word is spoken it cannot be retrieved, canceled, undone, or annulled. Isaac had given his blessing to

Jacob, and what was done was done. Which brings us right back to the sad sentence with which we began. Esau, with bitter tears clinging to his whiskers, with trembling hands clinging to his father, cried, "But don't you have a blessing for me, also? Bless me, too, Father. Bless me, too."

The blessing for which Jacob lied and for which Esau cried was a two-sided gift. On one side, it was a binding word of material blessing, and in that regard it functioned not unlike a will or estate plan. But, in addition to the bestowal of property and possessions, the other side of the parents' blessing meant approval and pride. In fact, the word translated "blessing" means, in the Hebrew language, "to speak well of or to praise."[2] For the child to receive the parents' blessing meant to have the parents' approval, to be spoken well of by the parents, to know that the parents found delight in the child.

That is the blessing for which Esau cried when he said, "What about me, Father? Don't you have any blessing left? Bless me, too, Dad. Bless me, too." And, ever since he said those words into the air, they have never fallen to the ground. The echo of Esau's cry has never known a homeless moment. Esau's echo has never lacked a lip on which to land, because everyone of us yearns to receive the blessing, to know that we are believed in, delighted in, and loved by our parents just for who we are. That isn't egotism or codependence or conceit. That's just the way God made us.

We all yearn, look, and listen for what the Bible calls "the blessing." We long to hear our parents "speak well of us," the literal meaning of the biblical word "blessing." We long to hear our parents say, "I love you, and I delight in you, and I am proud of you, not for anything you have achieved or accomplished, but just because of who you are. I expect you to do and be your best. Through discipline and guidance, I will draw boundaries for your behavior, and those boundaries will have to be obeyed. But I also want you to know that my love for you is not contingent upon how well you perform or how much you accomplish. I love you, and I delight in you, and I am proud of you, not because of what you have done, but because of who you are. So do right, be your best, and strive your hardest, but always remember that, no matter where you go or what you do, good or bad, right or wrong, your parents love you."

Something like that, said out loud, is at least a part of what it means to give a child the "blessing." To bless the child is to speak well of the child, to give the child the gift of unconditional love, the gift that the New Testament calls "grace." That is the blessing for which every listening ear and hungry heart is waiting. Everybody waits to receive "the blessing," the gift of knowing that they are loved with no strings attached. The hunger to be blessed is the common yearning of every heart. Whether or not that hunger is satisfied is one of the most critical factors in every person's life. Our lives are shaped and colored by the presence, or absence, of "the blessing." It is a blessing that has to be heard, so it is a blessing that must be said. Someone has to say the blessing out loud. But, all too often, the blessing never gets said.

Many parents, in a sincere, well-intentioned effort to "keep the children motivated," never quite come out and say the blessing. That doesn't mean they are bad parents. No, not at all. They may be very good parents who provide for their children, love them, nurture them, educate them, and support them. It's just that they are afraid to go ahead and tell their children that they love them unconditionally, no matter what. The parents are afraid that if they actually tell the children that they delight in them and are proud of them without regard for their achievements or accomplishments, then the children might lose their incentive to keep striving for excellence. This comes from a sincere fear that if you go ahead and tell the children that you delight in them, no matter what, then they'll stop studying and stop behaving and stop striving to please you, because they now know that your love for them is not at all contingent upon how well they perform. That assumption is based on the idea that children's real incentive to do right is their desire to earn their parents' smile, and if you go ahead and let the children know that they already have your smile, they'll quit trying to earn it, and they will have lost their motivation to succeed.

That view of life manifests itself in practical, little, everyday ways. The parent never says, "I am so proud of you," unless the child has just achieved an enormous accomplishment. The parent looks at a report card with several As and B's and one D, and all the conversation is critical of the D, with only passing mention of the A's and B's because, "If you praise them, they might get complacent." The parents, meaning well, with only the best of intentions, always hold the blessing slightly out of reach, because they honestly believe that is the best way to keep the child striving and stretching. In their hearts, they do love the child, no strings attached. In their hearts, they do love the child unconditionally. But they would never say that to the child, lest the child stop trying to earn their favor, win their approval, and gain their smile. They may be very good parents. They love, nurture, and educate their children. But they can't quite bring themselves to go ahead and give their son or daughter the free, unconditional gift of "the blessing," said out loud, no strings attached. "The blessing" never gets said, and the silence of the unsaid blessing is loud in the ears of the child, long after that child is grown up.

You can hear the loud, lingering silence of the unsaid blessing in a beautiful ballad from the famous twentieth-century American poet Reba McEntire, a ballad that travels under the haunting name, "The Greatest Man I Never Knew."

> The greatest man I never knew
> Lived just down the hall.
> And every day we said, "Hello,"
> But never touched at all.
> He was in his paper,
> I was in my room.
> How was I to know
> He thought I hung the moon?
>
> The greatest words I never heard,
> I guess I'll never hear.
> The man I thought would never die,
> Has been dead almost a year.

> He was good at business,
> But there was business yet to do.
> He never said he loved me,
> I guess he thought I knew.³

Many parents think their kid "hung the moon," but too many kids don't know it because the parents haven't said "the blessing" out loud. The greatest words a son or daughter can hear are the words that let them know that they have their parents' blessing of unconditional love. But for many sons and daughters, those are "the greatest words they've never heard" because those words of blessing are the words their parents have never said out loud. Children can't hear what their parents don't say. There are too many children who have never quite heard "the blessing," because there are too many parents who have never quite said it out loud.

And it usually isn't the parents' fault. They, themselves, may have grown up in a home where they never heard "the blessing." Their parents may never have said to them, "My love for you and my delight in you are not contingent upon how well you perform and how much you accomplish. I expect you to be your best and do your best. But I also want you to know that no matter what, no strings attached, I love you." If a person has never heard those words, it can be mighty hard for that person to say those words. After all, it is hard to give a gift you've never received.

So, generation after generation, parents withhold the blessing from their children. And the children grow up without quite receiving the blessing. So they spend their adult life still trying to "make Mama and Daddy proud." Now, they are all grown up, but they are still thinking, "Bless me, Daddy. Bless me, Mama. Tell me you're proud of me and that you delight in me, not because of something I've done, but just because of who I am." The absence of that blessing makes it hard for adult children to give the blessing to their own children, because it's hard to give a gift that you, yourself, have never received.

So, the next generation grows up with the blessing always held slightly out of reach, and then they relate to their children in the same way, and the cycle goes on, everybody loving everybody but nobody daring ever really to say it out loud in all of its unconditional, no-strings-attached, no-matter-what grace. And, all of a sudden, those strange, old, odd-sounding verses from the Old Testament don't sound so strange anymore, do they? You know, the verses that say, "The sins of the fathers will be visited on the third and fourth generation," and "The parents ate bitter grapes, and the children's teeth were set on edge." (The Bible gets smarter every day, doesn't it?)

So . . . how do you break the cycle? How can someone who is unable to say the blessing because they have never heard the blessing finally get the blessing so they can give the blessing? How is the cycle of the withheld blessing finally broken? Well, it isn't broken by making everybody feel guilty because they didn't do a perfect job of parenting, that's for sure. There are no perfect parents. Nobody gets it all just right. So, trying to see how guilty everybody can feel is an absolute waste. The cycle of the withheld blessing is not broken by parental feelings of guilt. Rather, the cycle of the withheld blessing is broken by an honest theology of grace. The good theology that embraces the radical, unconditional grace of God is what finally breaks the cycle of the withheld blessing.

Once you and I understand that God's settled posture toward us is that unconditional love that the Bible calls "grace," then we are at the beginning of the end of the cycle of the withheld blessing. The word grace comes from the Greek word *charis*, which means "gift." Gifts can never be earned, only given. God gives us God's love, not because we are good, but because God is good. You must know that you are the object of God's gift of love, the gift that cannot be earned but can only be received, the gift that we have come to call "grace."

That is what Jesus was talking about when he told that parable in Matthew 20, the one about the workers who all got paid the same, though some earned it and some didn't. That parable is the most radical statement of God's grace in the whole Bible. Grace rises to her highest crescendo at the end of the parable, where the farmer who is paying the workers, in response to those who begrudged his generosity, said those unforgettable words, "Are you angry because I am good? I can be as good as I please to whomever I please." That is the most radical statement of grace in all the Bible. "God can be as good as God pleases to whomever God chooses to give the blessing." That is grace . . . God's love for you and me, no matter what.

Once you hear that at the center of your soul and believe it for yourself, you don't lose your incentive to live a moral, pure, honest, innocent life. You don't become nonchalant about serving God and following Jesus and helping others, because you now know you don't have to earn God's favor. To the contrary, once you hear, really hear, and believe the gospel of grace, you are so filled with grateful wonder at God's unconditional love for you that all you want to do is to please God, not so you can get God's smile, but because you have God's smile. You need no external incentive, no promise of reward, no threat of punishment. You just love God because God first loved you.

You are free to just love God for nothing, because you now know that God loves you, for nothing! And it is then and there that the cycle of the withheld blessing begins to be broken. You are now free to give unconditional love to others, because you have finally received it for yourself. You are finally able to say the blessing out loud, because you have heard the blessing deep down. The good theology of grace can set you free to give your child the blessing. It can set you free from the insecurity that always made you see everyone else as a rival. It can set you free from always keeping score on everybody else because you now know that God is not keeping score on you.

Perhaps you have long been Esau's silent partner in that sad duet, "Bless me, too. Don't you have a blessing for me? Bless me, too, Mama. Bless me, too, Daddy." Good theology doesn't, all of a sudden, fix all of that. It is only a place to start. But it is the only place to start.

So, start here: Start with the sound theology of the gospel, the sound theology that says God is for you and God is with you. You are the object of God's unconditional love. It is called grace, and it is the ultimate blessing. It is the blessing that must be said, because it is the blessing that must be heard, trusted, and believed. Hear the blessing. Trust the blessing. Believe the blessing. Then, once you have heard, trusted, and believed the blessing, you will finally be free to say the blessing. Someone you know is dying to hear it. So say it. Please, someone say the blessing! Amen.

As soon as Isaac had finished blessing Jacob, when Jacob had scarcely gone out from the presence of his father Isaac, his brother Esau came in from his hunting. He also prepared savory food, and brought it to his father. And he said to his father, "Let my father sit up and eat of his son's game, so that you may bless me."

His father Isaac said to him, "Who are you?"

He answered, "I am your firstborn son, Esau."

Then Isaac trembled violently, and said, "Who was it then that hunted game and brought it to me, and I ate it all before you came, and I have blessed him?—yes, and blessed he shall be!"

When Esau heard his father's words, he cried out with an exceedingly great and bitter cry, and said to his father, "Bless me also, father!"

But he said, "Your brother came deceitfully, and he has taken away your blessing."

Esau said, "Is he not rightly named Jacob? For he has supplanted me these two times. He took away my birthright; and look, now he has taken away my blessing." Then he said, "Have you not reserved a blessing for me?"

Isaac answered Esau, "I have already made him your lord, and I have given him all his brothers as servants, and with grain and wine I have sustained him. What then can I do for you, my son?"

Esau said to his father, "Have you only one blessing, father? Bless me, me also, father!" And Esau lifted up his voice and wept.
—Genesis 27:30-38

For the kingdom of heaven is like a landowner who went out early in the morning to hire laborers for his vineyard. After agreeing with the laborers for the usual daily wage, he sent them into his vineyard.

When he went out about nine o'clock, he saw others standing idle in the marketplace; and he said to them, "You also go into the vineyard, and I will pay you whatever is right." So they went.

When he went out again about noon and about three o'clock, he did the same. And about five o'clock he went out and found others standing around; and he said to them, "Why are you standing here idle all day?"

They said to him, "Because no one has hired us."

He said to them, "You also go into the vineyard."

When evening came, the owner of the vineyard said to his manager, "Call the laborers and give them their pay, beginning with the last and then going to the first."

When those hired about five o'clock came, each of them received the usual daily wage. Now when the first came, they thought they would receive more; but each of them also received the usual daily wage. And when they received it, they grumbled against the landowner, saying, "These last worked only one hour, and you have made them equal to us who have borne the burden of the day and the scorching heat."

But he replied to one of them, "Friend, I am doing you no wrong; did you not agree with me for the usual daily wage? Take what belongs to you and go; I choose to give to this last the same as I give to you. Am I not allowed to do what I choose with what belongs to me? Or are you envious because I am generous?"

—Matthew 20:1-15

The parents say they have not given their children the blessing because the children are so difficult. Might it be that the children are so difficult because the parents have not given them the blessing?
—*Anonymous*

When a Family Moves

The pain that many families have felt on moving day has seldom been captured more softly and tenderly than it is in the first verse of a simple ballad made famous by Patty Loveless. It goes like this:

> Through the back window of our '59 wagon
> I watched my best friend Jamie slipping further away.
> I kept on waving till I couldn't see her,
> And my tears I asked again why we couldn't stay.
> Mama whispered softly, Time will ease your pain.
> Life's about changing, nothing ever stays the same.
> And she said,
> How can I help you to say "Goodbye"?
> It's okay to hurt, and it's okay to cry.
> Come let me hold you, and I will try.
> How can I help you to say "Goodbye"?[4]

Anyone who has ever left a beloved home to move to a distant place can find their own ache somewhere inside the frame of those insightful lines. It does, indeed, hurt to watch your familiar world fade from sight in the rearview mirror of a moving van. The only thing more painful is to watch your children watch their familiar world fade from sight with the last wave goodbye.

The pain of moving from the familiar and comfortable to the distant and strange is severe, but it is not uncommon. Most of us, somewhere along the way, will either wave goodbye from a moving van or to a moving van. Each year in the United States, there are about sixteen million moves that relocate about forty million persons, making the moving business a seven-billion-dollar-a-year industry.[5] If you add up those statistics, the sum of it all is this: Most of us, somewhere along the way, will wave goodbye from, or to, a moving van. (No wonder so many are so moved by that piercing pair of simple lines from Carole King's haunting song, "You're so far away. Doesn't anybody stay in one place anymore?")

Why are so many people moving? Where are they going? Why can't they stay? Well, needless to say, sometimes when a family moves it is because they have no other choice. Most often, that kind of "mandatory" move is precipitated by a job transfer. In theory, one can easily say, "Well, I just wouldn't move. I'd find another job before I would uproot my family." That is easy to say in the abstract. But, faced with the real choice between moving to a new place or losing employment, most people discover that economic necessity and financial reality leave them no option. So they move their family, because they must. They move in the summer, or in the middle of the school year. They move their children at a "good time" (when the child is a preschooler), or they move their children at a "bad time" (grade-schooler, middle-schooler, high-schooler). They have little control over when they move, scarce control over where they move, and even less control over whether they move. Sometimes families move because they must. It often hurts. It is frequently hard. And it happens somewhere every day.

Then, there are those families who move for less obvious, more ill-defined, and intangible reasons than the corporate transfer that leaves no choice. Mother or father feels an inescapable sense of need to move near their aging parents who live four states away. Husband or wife feels an insatiable sense of call to go to medical school or law school or theology school or some other graduate institution that is in a distant place. One or the other spouse, or both, feels an undeniable tug to go serve as a missionary or minister in a foreign nation or a faraway city. It is not something that they must do or lose their present job. (In fact, doing it will cause them to lose their present job!) It is altogether different from the corporate transfer. It is a move that is much more difficult to explain or define or, perhaps, defend. It is a move made in response to the tug of God, which is seldom as unambiguous and audible as a corporate transfer! I call it "moving by compelling choice." It is a "chosen move," but the choice was compelled by an undeniable tug. It is "moving by compelling choice."

It is hard to say which is more difficult for parents who must take their children away from the familiar and move them to a strange new place: the helpless feeling of *having to move* in order to keep a job or the guilty feeling of *choosing to move* in order to obey a tug. Which is worse? I don't know. If a company requires you to relocate, you have someone "to blame" for the pain of the move. But when you move in response to a relentless tug that you believe to be the call of God, there is no one "to blame." It's just you, trying to interpret God's tug and explain it to others, when you don't even fully understand it yourself.

We encounter in the pages of scripture a couple of rather conspicuous cases of families who moved to a new place in response to a compelling tug, a tug that was as difficult to explain as it was impossible to deny. The first case is one of the most familiar family relocations of them all, the story of Abraham and Sarah. Abraham and Sarah made one of those "moves by compelling choice." They chose to move, but their choice was compelled by an undeniable tug. This is how their tug to move is reported in the book of Genesis:

> Now the Lord said to Abram, Go from your country and your kindred and your father's house to the land that I will show you. I will make of you a great nation, and I will bless you, and make your name great, so that you will be a blessing. I will bless those who bless you, and the one who curses you I will curse; and in you all the families of the earth shall be blessed. So Abram went, as the Lord had told him. (12:1-4a)

That is a lean account of a family who felt compelled to move. Even for a time when nomadic movement was not uncommon, the description seems a bit lean and spare: "God said, Go from your country and your kindred and your father's house to the land that I will show you. . . . So Abram went, as the Lord had told him." If Abraham and Sarah were leaving behind all that was familiar ("go from your country and your kindred and your father's house") to strike out for parts unknown ("to the land that I will show you"), then you have to wonder how much uncertainty, ambiguity, doubt, and fear are traveling in the trunk of that lean, spare account: "God said go, so Abram went." After all, Abraham and Sarah were losing their home place and their familiar world. They couldn't even leave a forwarding address. The writer of the New Testament book of Hebrews summed it up with that unforgettable assessment, "By faith Abraham obeyed when he was called to set out . . . and he set out, not knowing where he was going" (11:8).

Now, you and I would like to think that, if someone is that obedient to God's tug, then surely God will grant them immediate success in their new endeavor as a "confirming sign" to assure them that they have done the right thing. Nothing, however, could have been further from the truth for Abraham and Sarah. If you read the Genesis account of their journey into the unknown, what you see is problem after problem . . . problems with Lot (their bothersome nephew), problems with Pharaoh (because he thought Sarah was so pretty she could make the stars fall from the sky!), problems with obtaining a piece of property (despite God's promise that they were venturing out to start a nation), and problems conceiving a child (despite God's prediction that their ancestors would be a countless clan).

Wherever the popular notion of "confirming signs" originated, it certainly was not a part of Abraham and Sarah's experience. Moving day placed them on a path made more for uncertain stumbling than for effortless gliding. Moving day was followed less by confirming signs than by exhausting complexities. Abraham and Sarah moved in response to a compelling tug, and it was the right thing for them to do. But, in their case, the right thing did not turn out to be the easy thing or the simple thing or the smooth thing. Indeed, moving in response to God's compelling tug put Abraham and Sarah on an uncertain path where there was little clear light and much dark shadow.

Which is not unlike the way it was for another Bible family who moved in response to a compelling tug. In fact, this family moved, and moved, and moved again. They are as famous a family to the New Testament as Abraham and Sarah are famous to the Old. Their names are Mary and Joseph and Jesus. Here is the way Matthew described their many moving days:

> An angel of the Lord appeared to Joseph in a dream and said, "Get up, take the child and his mother, and flee to Egypt, and remain there until I tell you; for Herod is about to search for the child, to destroy him." Then Joseph got up, took the child and his mother by night, and went to Egypt, and remained there until the death of Herod. . . . Herod . . . killed all the children in and around Bethlehem who were two years old or under. . . . When Herod died, an angel of

the Lord suddenly appeared in a dream to Joseph in Egypt and said, "Get up, take the child and his mother, and go to the land of Israel, for those who were seeking the child's life are dead." Then Joseph got up, took the child and his mother, and went to the land of Israel. But when he heard that Archelaus was ruling over Judea in place of his father Herod, he was afraid to go there. And after being warned in a dream, he went away to the district of Galilee. There he made his home in a town called Nazareth. (2:13-23)

Poor Joseph and Mary . . . So many hard decisions . . . So many unexpected problems . . . So many moving days . . . So many strange places. This was not at all the way they had imagined life would be. Life was not turning out at all the way they had it planned. They never dreamed that other babies would be buried in Bethlehem just because their baby was born in Bethlehem. They never dreamed that they would have to keep moving from place to place, trying to find a place where they could raise this special child and be a normal family. So much fear . . . So much uncertainty . . . So much moving around from place to place.

And the fact that, sixty or seventy years later, the writer of the Gospel of Matthew could reflect on all of this as the fulfillment of prophecy should not lead us to think that, as all of this was unfolding, Joseph and Mary were looking at it that way. Matthew got to write about it after it happened, but Joseph and Mary had to live through it as it happened. What they found themselves living through was a series of difficult moving days.

They moved in response to a compelling tug. And, though they were surely the most special and blessed family in the whole Bible, even they struggled to know God's will and, at least once, seemed to have made a serious mistake in their efforts to discern God's tug to move. After all, Joseph's dream said that, now that Herod was dead, the danger was past and Joseph and Mary could return home with the little boy Jesus. And yet, when they got to the state line, thinking they were following God's tug, they discovered that Herod's successor, Archelaus, was even more dangerous than Herod.

So that move didn't work out. What had felt like the right move for their family turned out all wrong. They had to look for another place. They had to make another move. And this is Joseph and Mary, mind you! God's most special family is stumbling through life, moving in response to compelling tugs that are seldom clear, never easy, and sometimes bewildering. In that sense, when Joseph and Mary move, they are not unlike Abraham and Sarah. They are moving in response to a compelling tug, but they seem mostly to be "going without knowing." All of which helps all of us who have ever made a difficult move to feel closer kin to those two families than ever we would have expected.

When families move, they struggle with a host of hard questions:

"Should we do this?"
"Is this the right thing?"
"Will we make friends there?"
"How will this move affect the children?"

"How long will it be before we move again?"

"Do you think this is God's will for our lives?"

When we face a family move, we face all those ambiguities and uncertainties that make us feel surprisingly close kin to Abraham and Sarah and Mary and Joseph, all of whom moved at God's tug and searched for God's will.

When it comes to knowing God's will and following God's tug, most of us are about like Abraham and Sarah, and Mary and Joseph. We have to go out "not knowing where we are going." We think, ponder, pray, and struggle our way through to a decision. We do our best. But "knowing God's will" often feels less like absolute certainty than a mysterious tug.

The ambiguity and uncertainty of our struggles to know and follow the tug of God are captured in a page from the prayer journal of Thomas Merton. Merton, that great spiritual guide and devotional thinker, once wrote the following prayer:

> My Lord God, I have no idea where I am going. I do not see the road ahead of me. I cannot know for certain where it will end. . . . And the fact that I think I am following your will does not mean that I am actually doing so. But I believe, dear Father, that the desire to please you does in fact please you, and I hope that I have that desire in all that I am doing. I hope that I will never do anything apart from that desire. And so I believe that if I do this, you will lead me by the right road, though I may know nothing about it.[6]

Merton loaned his voice to countless struggling souls when he prayed, "My Lord God, I have no idea where I am going. I do not see the road ahead of me. I cannot know for certain where it will end. . . . And the fact that I think I am following your will does not mean that I am actually doing so." With those words, Merton spoke for many families who have had to move from a familiar home to a distant place.

We never really know how a move will unfold. We have no way of knowing whether or not we will find good new friends in the strange new place. And we cannot know ahead of time how the move will affect our children. (Indeed, we probably won't even know at the time how the move is affecting our children. That is something we may not know until years later.) The popular colloquialism is accurate: "Life can only be lived forward and understood backward." The old gospel song is correct: "Farther along we'll know more about it." For now, we simply have to do our best and trust our future and our children to the grace and love of God. For now, we can only pray for the light we need to make the right choices when we are faced with "a mandatory move" or "a move by compelling choice." And, even with our most diligent efforts, our most honest prayers, and our most thoughtful search for the truth, we still may make our move with great ambiguity, uncertainty, and fear.

And what then? What should we do if an approaching move brings sorrow and fear to someone, or everyone, in the family? This much is clear: Everyone in the family should be honest with one another about the feelings that are fermenting inside them as moving day draws near. If children are school-age or older, they may be worried or sad about leaving their familiar home and moving to a strange place. If so, then the children will be helped, not hurt, by knowing that their parents share their pain at the prospect of being uprooted from a beloved neighborhood and friends to go to a new home that is distant and unknown. That kind of pain is a family kind of ache, the family kind of ache that binds families together rather than pulling families apart.

Sometimes, moving day is an exciting day for everyone, or someone, in the family. If it is a happy day, the joy does not need to be disguised. But, sometimes, moving day is a heartbreaking day for everyone, or someone, in the family. If it is a sad day, the pain does not need to be denied. It is alright for the children to know how their parents feel about the move—good or bad, happy or sad, worried or secure. It is, indeed, more than alright. It is healthy, honest, true, and good. When a family is facing moving day, the people in that family are bound together, not by the feelings they hide, but by the feelings they share . . . even if they share them through tears falling into half-packed boxes half-full of half-wrapped dishes.

Somewhere along the way, Anne Murray sang a song called "Somebody's Always Saying Goodbye." She was right, of course. Somebody somewhere is always saying goodbye to someplace familiar and old on their way to someplace distant and new. It happens to somebody, somewhere, everyday. Most of us will someday find ourselves being that somebody who is saying goodbye.

When we move, either because "we have to" or because "we choose to," it will likely be with some uncertainty, some fear, some mystery, and some pain. We may not get "confirming signs of success." (Abraham and Sarah didn't; nor did Joseph and Mary.) We may not be able to say with unwavering certainty, "This is the will of God." (That conclusion usually comes much later, farther along, after life has had a chance to unfold.) And, it may not "work out" and "feel good" for the whole family.

Those are the honest realities we face when we move. I wish it was neater, nicer, cleaner, and easier. But it isn't. (Remember Abraham and Sarah! Remember Joseph and Mary!) The fact is, while moving is sometimes exciting, happy, and wonderful, moving, more often, is frightening, sad, and painful. But, by the grace of God, we live through the most difficult moving days. We learn to find new joys in strange places. And we discover that we can never move anywhere that is beyond the sustaining presence of the God who tugs at us and goes with us, no matter where we have to, or choose to, move. Amen.

By faith Abraham obeyed when he was called to set out . . . and he set out, not knowing where he was going.

—*Hebrews 11:8*

Letting Go and Going On

When I was a boy, we always had a huge garden out behind our house. My father was a very gifted weekend farmer who grew the world's best potatoes and cucumbers. Every spring at pea-planting time, he would stir me from my slumber early on Saturday mornings so that he could share with me the joys of tilling the soil. But, sad to say, around our place the soil got tilled, not by a tractor or even a gas-powered rotary tiller, but by that most primitive and unforgiving implement known to the human race: the push-plow. (For the agriculturally uninitiated, a push-plow consists of one skinny metal wheel attached to two long wooden handles, bearing a pie-shaped plow blade and no motor!)

My father could push-plow a pea-row straighter than a hair-part on a Brylcream billboard without ever so much as taking a deep breath, while I, on the other hand, would weave my way from one end of the garden to the other, leaving in my wobbly wake a row so crooked that, once, when we ate too many of the peas that grew in my row, they actually made us dizzy and left us staggering about, unsteady on our feet. Whenever I would ask my father why his rows were straight as an arrow while mine were crooked as a snake, he would always give the same reply: "Son, when I plow, I look way out to the end of the row and plow to where I'm going, while you, on the other hand, are always looking back to see where you've already been. You can't plow straight looking back."

My father's philosophy on pea-row plowing was sleeping deep inside my memory in some long-forgotten corner until it was one day roused from hibernation by that strange old Bible verse in the Gospel of Luke, the one in which Jesus says, "No one who puts a hand to the plow and looks back is fit for the kingdom of God" (9:62). Whatever else that verse means, it at least seems to indicate that Jesus was not too big on the backward look. Jesus seems to have taken a rather dim view of the backward look that leaves us paralyzed by the pull of the past. Jesus' words put him clearly on the side of letting go and going on.

That, of course, does not mean that there is no place in life for memory. To the contrary, memory is one of God's dearest gifts to us. The old pictures, the saved letters, the home place, the friend long unseen but never forgotten—these are gifts of God's grace. To remember and to be remembered can even be the thing that keeps us most alive when we face difficult times in distant places. The most beautiful and powerful words about memory that I have ever encountered are in the little book *Whistling in the Dark*, where Frederick Buechner writes:

> When you remember me, it means that you have carried something of who I am with you, that I have left some mark of who I am on who you are. It means that you can summon me back to your mind even though countless years and miles may stand between us. It means that if we meet again, you will know me. It means that even after I die, you can still see my face and hear my voice and speak to me in your heart. For as long as you remember me, I am never entirely lost. If you forget me, part of who I am will be gone.[7]

Buechner's words ring true. It is a wonderful gift and a beautiful thing to remember and to be remembered. Memories are among God's dearest gifts.

Jesus, I am quite sure, is not admonishing us to forget our memories when he speaks of the peril of looking back. Rather, Jesus is calling us to come to terms with the reality that life can only be lived forward. We must not turn back to old security because we fear the uncertainty ahead. We must not waste our lives in a futile effort to recapture, relive, or redo that which is over. We have to let go, go on, and live fully into whatever is coming next.

That seems to be what Paul was saying when he wrote to the Philippians, "Forgetting the past, I press forward." When Paul uses the phrase, "forgetting the past," he is not talking about erasing the past from his memory. Rather, Paul is talking about letting go of his past, not allowing his past to paralyze him and keep him from going forward and living into the future.

For several years now, I have been unable to read Paul's Philippian confession about forgetting the past and pressing on to the future without hearing, in the distant background, a faint echo from, of all places, a baseball locker room. It happened in September of 1987. The California Angels were locked in a fierce battle for first place in the Western Division of the American League. There was less than a week left in the season, and every single game had become bigger than life itself. In one of those critical last games, the Angels had a seemingly insurmountable lead going into the late innings, only to blow the lead and lose the game. It was a crushing defeat that dealt a crippling blow to the Angels' pennant hopes. After the game, a sportswriter made his way through the silent, somber locker room to talk with one of the Angels' star players, a veteran of many seasons. The sportswriter said, "Well, I guess that must be one of the most bitter losses of your entire career," to which the player responded, with quiet wisdom and unforgettable insight, "Yes. It was a difficult and disappointing loss, and it hurts. But that one is over now, and we'll just have to stop wanting that one."[8]

"That one is over now, and we'll just have to stop wanting that one." Whenever I hear Paul say, "Forgetting the things that are behind, I press on to the things that are ahead," I hear the echo of those simple words of that athlete. There are some things in life that are over. And when they are over, we have to let them go and let them be over. All of which is sort of like what C. S. Lewis once said:

> The one prayer God will never answer is the prayer for an encore. God's creativity is much too vast for that. God simply will not give us back the good old days. Rather, God will give us good new days.[9]

If you take all those words and add them together, the sum of it all is this: Life does not come with a rewind button. We don't get to undo decisions, relive moments, or recapture days. (There was a time in my life when I thought the slipperiest thing in the world was a catfish right after you pulled it from the pond and just before you dropped it in the bucket. But now I know better. Now I know that the most slippery, hard-to-hold-onto thing on the face of the earth is a page from last year's calendar. Life won't let you hold onto a day that is gone. You cannot hold onto last year's calendar. It will slip out of your hands. It may be hard to let go of last year's calendar, but it is even harder to hold onto it. You can't hold onto last year's calendar. You can look back through its pages and remember its moments. But you can't hold onto it. It will slip through your hands every time.)

All of us have moments we wish we could relive. We have all made decisions we wish we could have back. We have all done things we wish we could undo or redo. But the path to which we have set our feet is not open in that direction. It is only open ahead. But, by the grace of God, it is always open ahead. We do get to start over, go forward, and begin again. Sometimes we just have to let go and go on. Our life is not "back there," wherever "there" was. Our lives are here, wherever "here" is. We are not somewhere else, somewhere "back there" or "back then." We are here. And it is here, wherever we now are, that we must live our lives. We can remember last year's calendar, but we cannot hold onto it. We must let go and go on. Amen.

When morning dawned, the angels urged Lot, saying, "Get up, take your wife and your two daughters who are here, or else you will be consumed in the punishment of the city."

When they had brought them outside, they said, "Flee for your life; do not look back or stop anywhere in the Plain; flee to the hills, or else you will be consumed."

But Lot's wife, behind him, looked back, and she became a pillar of salt.
—*Genesis 19:15, 17, 26*

*No one who puts a hand to the plow
and looks back is fit for the kingdom of God.*
—*Luke 9:62*

Break, break, break
At the foot of thy crags, O Sea.
The tender grace of a day that is dead
Will never come back to me.
—*Alfred Tennyson*

You Are Here

In the first weeks after we moved to Washington, I gained a whole new affection for, and appreciation of, maps. I grew especially fond of maps that have those little arrows on them, those arrows that point to the spot where you are and say, "You Are Here."

I once found those words to be a bit redundant. When I saw the words "You Are Here" on a map or a directory, I would talk back to them. "Well, of course, I am here," I would mutter. "I wouldn't be reading this if I wasn't here, because I'd be somewhere else. I don't need some little sign to tell me I am here. I know I am here." That's what I used to say to those "You Are Here" indicators. But never again. You won't hear me talking back to any more "You Are Here" signs. I have learned to love those words, "You Are Here."

My conversion came in a huge metropolitan hospital I had never before visited. When I asked directions to a patient's room, the person at the information desk handed me a map. It was a nice enough map, with buildings and corridors neatly sketched and drawn to scale. But it did not help me a whole lot, because it lacked one thing. What it lacked was one of those little arrows that points to a spot and says, "You Are Here." So I put the map down on the information desk and said to the person, "I see where I need to go, but I don't know how to get there from here, because I'm not exactly sure where 'here' is. Can you tell me where I am, right now?" She took a pencil, made a dot on the map, and said, "You are here."

"You are here." That phrase lands pretty near to the words that Jeremiah wrote to his friends who had been carried away captive and were living as exiles in Babylon. In his letter to the exiles, Jeremiah said, "You are here. Come to terms with the reality you face. You've bumped up against something painful that you cannot change. So you might as well live into it as fully as you can. Because, the fact is, you are here. This is your life. You are here."

That was Jeremiah's message to the exiled people of God. The story of the exile is that long, sad chapter in Judah's history, the chapter that began in 598 B.C. when Nebuchadnezzar and his army came and carried away a portion of the people of God. Nebuchadnezzar took them by force, seized them as captives, and deported them as exiles. He uprooted them from their homeland and carried them away to the strange land of Babylon.

But Nebuchadnezzar did not take all the people of God as exiles to Babylon. Among the remnant who were left behind was the prophet Jeremiah. Word got back to Jeremiah that the families who had been carried away in the exile were not doing so well adjusting to their strange new home. A part of the problem, apparently, was that they had not come to terms with the reality that their time in Babylon was going to last a while and they may as well make the best of it.

Jeremiah's letter is a powerful word for anybody who has ever had to live with something they could not change. What he said to the exiles was this:

> Thus says the Lord of hosts, the God of Israel, to all the exiles whom I have sent into exile from Jerusalem to Babylon: Build houses and live in them; plant gardens and eat what they produce. Take wives and have sons and daughters; take wives for your sons, and give your daughters in marriage, that they may bear sons and daughters; multiply there, and do not decrease. But seek the welfare of the city where I have sent you into exile. . . .
>
> Thus says the Lord: Only when Babylon's seventy years are completed will I visit you, and I will fulfill to you my promise and bring you back to this place. For surely I know the plans I have for you, says the Lord, plans for your welfare and not for harm, to give you a future with hope. (29:4-7a, 10-11)

With those words, the prophet Jeremiah called on the exiled people of God to come to terms with the fact that they were going to be in exile for a long time. He called on them to get on with their lives rather than being paralyzed by their despair over the way life had turned out for them. He reminded them that they must not put life on hold until the exile ended and they were safely back home. "Rather," he said, "Go ahead and build a house in Babylon. Go ahead and plant a garden in Babylon. Go ahead and raise your family in Babylon." What Jeremiah said to the exiles was this: "You are here. This may not be the way you had hoped life would turn out. This may not be the way you had assumed life would unfold. But this is your life. You are here. And while you are here you must live life fully, because the time of your life is passing by, and if you just keep putting your life on hold, trying to rewind it to the past or fast-forward it to the future, then your whole life is going to pass you by. You are here, and here is where you will have to find meaning and purpose and joy, or you will never find it anywhere!"

That was the message Jeremiah mailed to the exiled people of God. It was a letter to some people for whom life had turned out all wrong. It was an invitation to make the best of a situation that could not be changed.

Jeremiah was right. We will all, somewhere along the way, find ourselves and our families living through something that will not budge or change or go away. It cannot be gotten around; it can only be lived through. Those times come to every family somewhere along the way. We don't get to choose the times. We only get to choose how we will respond to them.

In that sense, we are not unlike Adam naming the animals in the garden of Eden. In Genesis 2, the Bible says that

> The Lord God formed every animal of the field . . . and brought them to the man to see what he would call them; and whatever the man called every living creature, that was its name. . . . The man gave names to . . . every animal of the field. (vv. 19, 20)

I never had thought much about that Bible verse until a few years ago when I ran across John Claypool's beautiful and powerful application of that little fragment of scripture to our complex and demanding lives.[10] Dr. Claypool observed that Adam did not get to create the animals; he only got to call them something when they came to him. Adam did not get to color or shape or design the animals; he only got to meet them and then respond to what he saw by giving them a name, by calling them something: elephant, chipmunk, aardvark, yard-dog, and so on. He did not get to choose the way the animals looked; he only got to respond to them by giving them a name.

And so it is with all of us. We don't get to choose the animals; we only get to name them. By and large, other than the problems we bring on ourselves by our poor choices, we don't have much power over which disappointments and struggles come our way. We don't get to pick them or shape them. They just come. And when they come, what you and I get to do with them is exactly what Adam got to do with the animals: We get to look our struggles in the face and give them a name. We get to respond to them by calling them something. We can call them the end of the world. We can say that life will never be happy or good again. We can invest our struggles and problems and sorrows with that much power, if we choose. We can shut down and close up and become bitter, brittle, and angry.

Or, we can respond to our struggles, problems, and sorrows in a different way. We can look our struggles in the face and give them a different name. We can say,

"This is an enormous difficulty that has come into our lives. This is not at all the way we had life planned. It hurts, and it is hard. But this is our life. We will have to go ahead and live our lives as fully and as faithfully as we can and let God wring whatever good can be wrung from these difficult days. By the grace of God and with the help of God, we will live into the pain of life, we will live through the pain of life, and we will live beyond the pain of life. We will not let this diminish, embitter, and destroy us. We will, instead, let this deepen and soften and enlarge us."

Like Adam in Eden, we don't get to shape the animals; we only get to name them. We don't get to choose the problems our families have to face; we only get to respond to them, call them something, and decide whether or not we will allow the pain to open us up to the presence of God.

Whatever your family is facing, the fact is, you are here. This is your life. Wherever you are, you are here. And here, today, is where you will have to find joy, meaning, and purpose if you are going to find it at all. You are here. You can't rewind life and recover a happier, easier time. You can't fast-forward life and skip over whatever you are having to face. And you can't afford to waste your life by putting it on hold "until things get back to normal" or "until we can get on with our life." You are "on with your life," because your life is going by, every day. As the famous Southern humorist Lewis Grizzard once said, "This ain't no dress rehearsal." He was right. No matter how difficult life may feel, no matter how unhappy our circumstances may be, the fact is, life itself, the only life we will ever have, is going by. This is not a dress rehearsal. This is life, and it is passing.

Your family may be struggling with something you never would have chosen. Your family may be bearing a burden you did not get to pick. Your family may be feeling captive to something that will not budge, change, or go away. Your family may be living in a hard place or going through a long struggle. You need to know that you are not alone. We are never alone, abandoned, forsaken, or forgotten. God is with us, and God somehow enables us to live through things that, if someone had told us we were going to have to endure, we would have sworn we could not have lived through them. But we do. By the grace and help of God, we stay on our feet, we keep moving, and we not only live through the struggle, but we might even emerge from it better than ever we would have been without it. That does not mean that God sends the struggle to make us better, but it does mean that when the struggle comes, it is God's nature to resurrect some surprising goodnesses from some dreadful darknesses.

Wherever you are, "you are here." But you are not here all by yourself. You are here. But so is God. God is with you, God is for you, and God will never leave you alone. Not even here. Especially not here, where you are. Amen.

These are the words of the letter that the prophet Jeremiah sent from Jerusalem to the remaining elders among the exiles, and to the priests, the prophets, and all the people, whom Nebuchadnezzar had taken into exile from Jerusalem to Babylon. This was after King Jeconiah, and the queen mother, the court officials, the leaders of Judah and Jerusalem, the artisans, and the smiths had departed from Jerusalem. The letter was sent by the hand of Elasah son of Shaphan and Gemariah son of Hilkiah, whom King Zedekiah of Judah sent to Babylon to King Nebuchadnezzar of Babylon.

It said: Thus says the Lord of hosts, the God of Israel, to all the exiles whom I have sent into exile from Jerusalem to Babylon: Build houses and live in them; plant gardens and eat what they produce. Take wives and have sons and daughters; take wives for your sons, and give your daughters in marriage, that they may bear sons and daughters; multiply there, and do not decrease. But seek the welfare of the city where I have sent you into exile, and pray to the Lord on its behalf, for in its welfare you will find your welfare. For thus says the Lord of hosts, the God of Israel: Do not let the prophets and the diviners who are among you deceive you, and do not listen to the dreams that they dream, for it is a lie that they are prophesying to you in my name; I did not send them, says the Lord.

For thus says the Lord: Only when Babylon's seventy years are completed will I visit you, and I

will fulfill to you my promise and bring you back to this place. For surely I know the plans I have for you, says the Lord, plans for your welfare and not for harm, to give you a future with hope.
—*Jeremiah 29:1-11*

When Is Enough Enough?

Long before anyone ever had much to say about the wisdom of recycling and the foolishness of littering, I learned an unforgettable lesson about the proper disposal of unwanted paper products. It happened one Saturday morning when I was six years old. My father had taken me with him to Holland's Market, a corner store with benches sitting in front, hams hanging in back, a stunningly beautiful display of Nehi grape and orange drinks, and what was reputed, by some of our more cosmopolitan and well-traveled neighbors, to be the most impressive array of Dr. Scholl's foot care products south of Atlanta.

While wandering about in that Neiman-Marcus of pedestrian accessories and culinary delights, I passionately entreated my father to buy me a candy bar. He did not always succumb to such trivial requests. But, on this day, much to my joy, he caved, and I returned to the car gleefully clutching that paragon of confectionery wonders, a Milky-Way. As we pulled out of the Holland's

Market parking lot, I eagerly tore off the wrapper and crumpled it into my pocket. That left me holding, in one hand, the candy bar, and, in the other hand, that little dark brown rectangular strip of cardboard that used to come in every candy bar wrapper. For some utterly inexplicable reason, instead of just putting the little strip of cardboard on the seat or in my pocket, I made the dreadful choice to throw it out the open window of our 1951 Plymouth.

That ill-advised decision soon issued in severe consequences. With the dark brown candy bar in one hand and the dark brown strip of cardboard in the other, I became confused, and, in a literal fulfillment of our Lord's command that "the right hand not know what the left hand is doing," I tossed from the car window, not the cardboard, but the candy bar! I realized immediately my dreadful mistake and turned around to gaze through the back windshield just in time to watch my erstwhile Milky-Way disappear beneath the left front tire of a pulpwood truck. It has since been thirty-five years. I don't recall what I got for Christmas that year or what I made on my report card. But I can still remember the awful empty feeling that swept over me when I realized that I had thrown away the very thing I wanted and that I was left with nothing.

I never think about that long-ago day in my little six-year-old life, except, of course, when I see a "Do Not Litter" sign, or when I eat a Milky-Way, or when I read the story of Adam and Eve. Almost every time I read about Adam and Eve, I remember the day I threw away the wrong thing, and the memory becomes a tiny parable of Adam and Eve who last saw the garden of Eden in the rearview mirror, through the back windshield, as they left behind all they ever wanted. They had thrown away the wrong thing, and it was gone, never to be retrieved.

Adam and Eve threw away the wonderful life they had because of a restless desire to have it all.[11] They already had all they could ever want or need. They had the whole garden of Eden. They had all of its space in which to live. They had all of its beauties at which to gaze. And they had all of its trees from which to eat. Well, almost all of its trees. There was this one tree in the middle of the garden that God had told Adam and Eve they could not have. And therein lay the problem. There was an off-limits tree. It was prohibited. It was the tree they could not have. And when the serpent pointed that out to them, it became, of course, the one tree they wanted most. The serpent said to Eve, "Did God tell you that this tree was off-limits? How unfair! God is just worried that if you eat from this tree you will know as much as God knows. God is trying to hold you back and keep you down."

Now, that, of course, is the point at which Eve and Adam could have said, "Oh no, God isn't that way at all. God has given us more trees than we can ever enjoy, more fruit than we can ever taste, more food than we can ever eat. We don't need to have that tree, because we already have all the trees we could ever want." That's what Eve and Adam could have said and should have said, and oh, if only that is what they would have said. But, instead, they began to grow restless with the limits God had given and the boundaries God had established. They became so focused on the one tree they could not have that they lost sight of the whole orchard they did have. They had more than enough, but, now, more than enough felt less than enough. If they could have the tree in the middle of the garden, then they could have it all! So they made their choice. They wanted to have it all. So they reached for the tree they could not have. And in their desire to have it all, they lost it all.

And there it is: the first sin . . . the sin of restless discontent. That was Adam and Eve's sin. They became discontented with the life God had given them. They wanted to have it all. And, irony of ironies, in their drive to have it all, they lost it all. When they reached for what they could not have, they threw away what they did have. Driven by restless discontent, Adam and Eve lost a life that was as good as life can get. Driven by restless discontent, they lost their capacity for seeing enough as being enough. Driven by restless discontent, they threw away a wonderful place and a happy life.

Adam and Eve have since had lots of children who have followed in their footsteps down the restless path of lifelong discontent. There is a name for that kind of restless discontent. I call it "the perilous lust for perfection." Everywhere I look, I see people who are being driven breathlessly, restlessly, angrily along by the perilous lust for perfection. Like Adam and Eve, they cannot ever bring themselves to say the word "enough." "We have enough." "Life is good enough." "Enough" simply is not in their vocabularies. They are driven by a restless discontentment that might best be described as "a perilous lust for perfection."

With this, of course, we must be careful, lest the perilous lust for perfection become confused with an honest need for change or a healthy quest for excellence. When people are trapped in dreadful circumstances or burdened by unbearable pain, their longing for relief is an honest need for change. And when people are striving to reach worthy goals and realize honorable ambitions, their passion for growth is a healthy quest for excellence. The honest need for change is real. The healthy quest for excellence is beautiful. They are not to be confused with the perilous lust for perfection. The perilous lust for perfection is neither the honest need for change or the healthy quest for excellence. The perilous lust for perfection is the kind of restless discontent that caused Adam and Eve to throw away the wrong thing. The perilous lust for perfection is the kind of restless discontent that simply cannot come to terms with the fact that life, even at its best, is only going to get so good.

For many families, the greatest enemy of peace and rest is the perilous lust for perfection. As long as you and I are demanding from human relationships and institutions a perfection that belongs to God and God alone, we will have no peace. We will forever be frustrated, restless, and discontented. There are no perfect families or marriages. There are no perfect husbands or wives or sons or daughters. There are no perfect friendships or jobs or churches. As long as you and I are looking for the perfect family or the perfect job or the perfect church, we will inevitably be restless, frustrated, and dissatisfied.

I have come to believe that there are few perils in life that are more destructive than that perilous lust for perfection that keeps so many families from ever knowing a quiet, settled, deep down sense of peace and contentment. And it isn't a rare or uncommon demon, this perilous lust for perfection. Rather, it is epidemic. In their perilous lust for perfection, countless people long to have it all. They yearn for life to be perfect. Thus, of course, nothing is ever quite good enough. The perilous lust for perfection, fed by unrealistic expectations, takes the phrase "the grass is always greener on the other side," and elevates it from a worn-out cliché to a deadly poison. The perilous lust for perfection causes families that could have been happy to throw away too much in a relentless quest for something more or someplace better.

We must somehow find that quiet, calm center where restless discontent is lost in the peace of God. We must learn how to say the word enough. We must learn to say no to restless discontent before it grows up to become the perilous lust for perfection. We must learn a few lessons from Adam and Eve in the shade of the tree at the center of the garden. The lessons are these:

Life, even at its best, only gets so good.
There are limits to be lived with,
because we cannot have it all.
Sometimes enough really is enough.

To learn these lessons is to find the opening of grown-up maturity and the beginning of deep-down peace.

Life, at its best, can be truly wonderful. But life, even at its best, is only going to get so good. To say that "life, even at its best, is only going to get so good" is not dark-eyed pessimism. It is, rather, clear-eyed realism. We must all come to terms with the fact that life, even at its best, is only going to get so good. Once we have embraced that truth, we can begin to live with realistic expectations, we can begin to feel a settled sense of contentment, we can begin, perhaps, even to be happy in a less-than-perfect place and, wonder of wonders, we might even learn how to say the most difficult to pronounce word in all the world: "Enough." Amen.

Now the serpent was more crafty than any other wild animal that the Lord God had made. He said to the woman, "Did God say, 'You shall not eat from any tree in the garden'?"

The woman said to the serpent, "We may eat of the fruit of the trees in the garden; but God said, 'You shall not eat of the fruit of the tree that is in the middle of the garden, nor shall you touch it, or you shall die.'"

But the serpent said to the woman, "You will not die; for God knows that when you eat of it your eyes will be opened, and you will be like God, knowing good and evil."

So when the woman saw that the tree was good for food, and that is was a delight to the eyes, and that the tree was to be desired to make one wise, she took of its fruit and ate; and she also gave some to her husband, who was with her, and he ate.

—Genesis 3:1-6

I have learned to be content with whatever I have.

—Philippians 4:11

Enough is so vast a sweetness,
I suppose it never occurs.

—Emily Dickinson

What Will the Children Remember?

Several years ago, someone put a newspaper clipping in my hand. When I unfolded it and saw that it was a column by that delightful humorist Erma Bombeck, I got ready to laugh. But, once I began reading her lines, I wanted less to laugh than to cry. Her words landed a little too close to home—too close to my home, and maybe too close to yours. The title of Erma Bombeck's column was "Time Through the Eyes of a Child," and this is what it said:

> When I was young,
>   Daddy was going to throw me in the air and catch me,
>   and I would giggle until I couldn't giggle anymore,
> but he had to change the furnace filter,
>   . . . so there wasn't time.

THE TUG OF HOME

When I was young,
    Mamma was going to read me a story,
    and I was going to turn the pages and pretend I could
        read,
but she had to wax the bathroom floor,
. . . so there wasn't time.

When I was young,
    Daddy was going to come to school and watch me in
        a play.
    I was the fourth Wise Man,
    just in case one of the other three got sick,
but he had an appointment,
    and it took longer than he thought,
. . . so there wasn't time.

When I was young,
    Mamma was going to listen to me read my essay on
    "What I Want to Be When I Grow Up,"
but she was in the middle of the Monday Night Movie,
    and Gregory Peck always was one of her favorites,
. . . so there wasn't time.

When I was young,
    Dad and I were going fishing one weekend, just the
        two of us,
    and we were going to pitch a tent and fry fish with
        the heads still on them,
    like they do in those flashlight commercials,
but at the last minute he had to fertilize the grass,
. . . so there wasn't time.

When I was young,
>   the whole family was going to pose together for our
>   Christmas cards,
> but my brother had ball practice,
>   my sister had her hair up,
>   Dad was watching the television,
>   and Mom had to wax the bathroom floor again,
> . . . so there wasn't time.[12]

Most of what Erma Bombeck wrote was pretty funny. But not this. It lands a little too close to home. And when it lands, it reminds us that when our children are all grown up, they won't be able to remember things that never happened. If there is something we would like for our children to someday remember, then we had better say that something or do that something because, when they are all grown up, the children will only be able to remember the words they actually heard and the things they really did.

Our children will not be able to remember something that never happened. When they are all grown up, they won't be able to remember that I sometimes rearranged my schedule just to go someplace with them if I never actually rearranged my schedule just to go someplace with them. They won't be able to remember that we often stopped for ice cream if we never actually stopped for ice cream. They won't be able to remember that we sometimes sat on the front steps on summer Saturday evenings and read the Sunday School lesson together unless we actually did it. They won't remember how it felt to hear their parents pray for them unless they actually heard it.

It sounds so elementary, obvious, and simple that to say it out loud sounds silly. But it is so true that it must be said. If there is something that we want for our children to someday remember, then we simply have to say it or do it. If you think it will someday be important for your children to remember that you read stories to them, then read stories to them, because they will not remember what they did not experience. If you think it will someday be important that your children remember hearing you pray for them, then pray for them, out loud, in their presence, because they will not remember what they did not hear. If you think it will someday be important for your children to remember that you played ball with them or baked muffins with them, then oil up your glove and grease down your pan, because they will not remember what they did not do.

I do not mean, by all of this, to suggest that parents can, or should, somehow fill their children's memories with nothing but sweetness and light. Nor do I mean to suggest that parents can, or should, take their children everyplace and give their children everything. But what I do mean to say is that if there are some things you think that you, and God, would want your children to someday remember, then you must say and do some of those things, because when your children are grown, they will only be able to remember *then* what they actually did and heard *now*. And the children won't be children for long, so you have to go ahead *now* and begin saying and doing what you want them to be able to remember *then*.

Toward the end of his stellar career, the great New York Yankees catcher, Yogi Berra, began to play in the outfield. He was not at all accustomed to the shadows that the late afternoon sunset cast across the outfield. As a catcher, he had always been the last person on the field to be in the shade. Now, out in left field, he was the first in the shadows. Reflecting on the quickly gathering shadows in the outfield, Berra coined one of his many famous "Yogi-isms" when he said, "It sure gets late early out there."[13]

Yogi was right. It does get late early. It gets real late, real early. Time passes. The years slip away. The children grow up. So, if there is something we want the children to someday remember, we must say it, if it can be said; we must do it, if it can be done; we must sing it, if it can be sung. Because, when the children are all grown up, they won't be able to remember the words they never heard, the things they never did, or the songs they never learned.

For parents and children, it gets late early. So, if there are children in the house, you might want to put down this book and go tell them something or do something with them, because the time is passing, the years are fleeting, and the children will not be able to remember the words they never heard and the things they never did. Amen.

I am reminded of your sincere faith, a faith that lived first in your grandmother Lois and your mother Eunice and now, I am sure, lives in you.

. . . But as for you, continue in what you have learned and firmly believed, knowing from whom you learned it, and how from childhood you have known the sacred writings that are able to instruct you for salvation through faith in Christ Jesus.
—*2 Timothy 1:5; 3:14-15*

When a Family Faces Death

There is only one experience that is the common possession of every family. There is only one reality that every family in all the world holds in common. That one single tie that binds each family to every other family is the inevitable reality of death. After all, not every family will have a baby. Not every family will own a house. Not every family will hold a job. Not every family will take a vacation or attend a graduation or enjoy a retirement. All of those events are familiar realities for many families, but none of them are universal realities for all families. The only common experience that touches every human family is the inevitable reality of death. Many families miss many experiences, but no family misses death, because death misses no family.

But, while every family is the same when it comes to death, every death is not the same when it comes to families. Some families will face the death of an aged loved one whose life has been diminished by advancing disease and failing health. Other families will face the death of a child or teenager who was full of life when death came. Other families will face the death of a middle-aged adult who precedes elderly parents to the grave. Every family is the same when it comes to death. But every death is not the same when it comes to families. What binds families together is the inevitable experience of death. But what sets families apart are the different ways in which, and the different times at which, death comes; sometimes to those who have lived a long life, for whom "death was expected," and sometimes to those who are yet young and healthy, for whom death came out of season, out of time, out of place.

Byron Herbert Reese was a hill country genius who wrote magnificent poems in the solitude of the North Georgia mountains. In one of his poems he came mighty close to putting a frame around the difference between an expected death and a shocking death, a death in season and a death out of season. The poem is called "Bitter Berry." It is about the imminent death of a young girl, the daughter of a Mr. Helmer:

> The voice of the water
> Crying on a stone
> Said to Helmer's daughter
> Sitting alone:
>
> "Death itself is mellow
> When age has ripened one,
> But death's a bitter berry
> In the morning of the sun."

> And so to Helmer's daughter
> The youngest one of all,
> The green untimely berry
> Was as bitter as gall.[14]

What Byron Herbert Reese said with his spare, simple ballad is not unlike a sentence from William Sloane Coffin's sermon, "Alex's Death," a message Dr. Coffin preached shortly after his young son died in a tragic accident. The grieving father said, When parents die . . . they take with them a large portion of the past. But when children die, they take away the future as well.[15] A farmer/poet in the North Georgia hills and a famous preacher in the middle of New York City are both saying the same thing, and what they are saying is something we have long known: Every family is the same when it comes to death, but every death is not the same when it comes to families.

When someone we love has been suffering for a long time, death can bring a sense of relief. If someone we love has been in agonizing pain, their death can feel like a gift, a blessing, a release, and a relief. If someone we love has not known anyone for years, if they have long been able only to lie in bed, powerless to turn over, hands bound to the railing so they won't pull on some sustaining tube, then death can bring a quiet sigh of relief. Which is not to say that the same death causes no sorrow and brings no grief. Indeed, what we discover is that we feel quiet relief and deep sorrow simultaneously. And, wonder of wonders, one of those emotions does not diminish the other.

God has given us the capacity to feel more than one emotion at a time, and to feel each emotion deeply and fully. If we feel a sense of relief when a long-suffering loved one dies, that sense of relief does not diminish our sadness that someone we love more than life itself is gone from us. On the other hand, our sadness that someone we love more than life itself is gone from us does not diminish our sense of relief. When a family faces the death of a long-suffering loved one, the relief we feel at the death does not subtract from the sorrow, and the sorrow we feel at the death does not subtract from the relief.

Here is a wonder that defies explanation and transcends reason: God has given us the capacity to feel relief and sorrow simultaneously, fully and completely without one numbing us to the other. What a wonder. What a gift, the wonderful gift of being able to feel fully everything we feel in the face of death. The stream of life in which we wade does flow with more than one current of emotion, and in the face of death, the currents of relief and sorrow can, and do, flow side by side, one as deep and strong as the other. So it is when death comes "in season" to one whose life has long been diminished by the loss of all awareness or by the agony of relentless suffering.

But that death is not the death that every family faces. Some families face a different death. Every death is the same. But every death is different. Death comes to some families when it is "expected to come." But some families face a different kind of death, the death of a child or a teenager or a young, healthy adult who is absolutely full of life when death comes. And then, there is no relief. There is, at that death, nothing about which to feel relief. There is, instead, shock, sorrow, anger, pain, and disbelief for families who must face the death of the young and strong whose lives end out of season, long too soon.

In the face of that death, the heart does break. It really does break. And when the heart really does break, we have to let it be as broken as it really is. There is not much good sense in the plastic mask of denial that seeks to rush past the heartbreak. When the heart breaks, we just have to let it be as broken as it is. It will begin to mend as time unfolds. By the grace of God, the hope of the gospel, the power of the resurrection, the love of friends, and the turning of the calendar, the broken heart will someday find itself mending. But there is no shortcut to someday. There aren't any bypasses around the brokenness. In a tender, beautiful corner of John's Gospel, Jesus eventually restored Lazarus to life. There was a new day coming. Everybody did live to laugh again. But first, Jesus wept. He cried. In the face of death and sorrow and who knows what all else he saw and felt, Jesus just stood there and cried.

The heart does break. You cannot see it break on an EKG or an MRI, but you can feel it break in your chest and your throat. Sometimes the death a family faces can cause the heart to break. Not always. Sometimes death comes so "in season" that deep sorrow and deep relief fill the heart but don't break it. But sometimes death comes so "out of season" that the heart does break. When those times come, we are afraid to let the heart be broken, because we don't know what to do in the face of that much pain. So we often start trying to cover the brokenness too soon with too many slogans and mottos and clichés. Better to wait. When the heart really is broken, better just to be close by, better just to stay near, better to withhold too much talk that tries to fix too much too soon. When the heart does break, we just have to let it be what it is, knowing that, by the grace of God, a mending time will begin in God's season.

Every family will face death. But not every family will face the same death. To some families, death will come after everyone has expected it for months. To other families, death will come before anyone expected it for years. For some families, an expected death will fill the heart with pain and relief. For other families, a shocking death will break the heart with pain and pain. But what all families must know is that when the heart is full and when the heart is broken, God is present, God is near, and God is enabling us to live in the face of death. When those we love more than life itself go to be where God is, God is where we are. When we commend those we love into God's strong hands, we are ourselves held in God's strong hands. We are not left alone to face death. God is with us. God is for us. God is holding us in God's strong hands, even, or especially, in the face of death. Amen.

Jesus wept.

Life,
In the Light of Death

It may be the most ironic of ironies. It might be the most paradoxical of paradoxes. It could be the most contradictory of contradictions. But it is, nonetheless, true: *We are never more fully alive than when we are living our lives in the light of our own death.*

It is true. It may be ironic, paradoxical, and contradictory. But it is also very, very true that we are never more fully alive than when we are living life in the light of the certainty of our own death. We never know fully how to love life deeply until we realize how precious an ordinary day of life is. And we never realize how precious an ordinary day of life is until we come to terms with the fact that the time of our life is limited. And we never come to terms with the fact that the time of our life is limited until we embrace the truth that someday is going to be the last day. And we never embrace the truth that someday is going to be the last day until we honestly face the fact that we really are going to die. Probably not today, hopefully not tomorrow, possibly not for years or even decades to come, but someday—some inevitable, eventual, inescapable, certain someday—we really are going to die.

Once we face the fact that we really are going to die, we are finally, really ready to live life and love life, because we know that if we are going to die, that means someday is going to be the last day. And if someday is going to be the last day, that means the time of our life is limited. And if the time of our life is limited, that means that even the most routine and ordinary day of life is precious. But we never reach those conclusions apart from a clear awareness of the certainty of our own death, what I call "living life in the light of death."

Here, of course, we must be careful. Living life in the *light* of death is a very different idea from living life in the *shadow* of death. To live life in the shadow of death would be to live our days morbid and fatalistic, preoccupied with the possibility of death. That is what it would mean to live life in the shadow of death. To live life in the shadow of death would be to fall prey to the sort of frantic now-or-never drivenness that has been called the "I'll die young script."[16]

To live life in the light of death is something altogether different from living life in the shadow of death. To live life in the shadow of death is to be paralyzed. To live life in the light of death is to be energized. When we live life in the light of the certainty of our own death, we develop a healthy sense of urgency—not "urgency" as in frantic, compulsive drivenness, but "urgency" as in sensitive awareness. We are never more fully alive than when we are aware of how limited, precious, and passing is the time of our lives. We never come to that awareness apart from a healthy, honest sensitivity to the certainty of our own death.

All of this talk about living life in the light of death is not an invitation for us to "live each day as though it will be our last." (The level of intensity that would require would not be easily sustained!) I am not suggesting that we engage in the frantic intensity of living each day as though it will be our last day. Rather, I am suggesting that we live each day as though someday will be the last day. That is what it means to live our lives in the light of death, energized by a sensitive awareness to the certainty of our own death. That sensitive awareness is the "healthy sense of urgency" we hear in the psalmist's prayer.

> Our years come to an end like a sigh. The days of our life are seventy years, or perhaps eighty, if we are strong; . . . they are soon gone, and we fly away. . . . So teach us to count our days that we may gain a wise heart. (Ps 90:9b-10, 12)

The psalmist is living life in the light of death, coming to terms with the fact that someday is going to be the last day, which means that everyday is precious.

Frederick Buechner captures all of this inside the striking fences of these insiqhtful sentences:

> [Today] is the point to which all your yesterdays have been leading since the hour of your birth. It is the point from which all your tomorrows will proceed until the hour of your death. If you were aware of how precious [today] is, you could hardly live through

it. Unless you are aware of how precious it is, you can hardly be said to be living at all.[17]

With those words, Buechner has come close to putting a frame around this unframeable truth, the truth about living our lives in the light of death, living lives energized by a sensitive awareness that someday will be the last day, which makes us see each day almost as precious as it really is. It rings true to us, deep down in our bones, when we read those stunning words: "If you were aware of how precious [today] is, you could hardly live through it. Unless you are aware of how precious it is, you can hardly be said to be living at all."

We must learn to do what the psalmist called "counting our days," which means we must learn to live our lives in the light of the certainty of our own death. Wonder of wonders, we are never more fully alive than when we are living in the light of death. We can see life for the fleeting, limited, precious gift that it is when we are looking at life in the light of the certainty of our own death. Isn't it odd? Isn't it strange? The clearest we ever see the sacredness of our own life is when we finally look at life in the light of the certainty of our own death. To look at life in the light of death is to finally recognize that even the most ordinary of life's moments is sacred and alive and fleeting.

In the last act of Thornton Wilder's powerful play, *Our Town*, his character Emily gets to "come back from the dead" for a day. She has recently died while giving birth to her second child. She watches her own funeral from the perspective of eternity. Then, she exercises her prerogative to "come back among the living" for a day.

The day Emily chooses to relive is her twelfth birthday. Thornton Wilder allows us to watch both Emily's visit back in time to when she was twelve and her reaction to it as she watches it all happen from the perspective of her new life in eternity. Now that she is looking at life in the light of her own death, she cannot bear the way "living people" rush through life, waste life, and miss the sacredness that is in the most ordinary moments. Finally, she decides she can't bear to be back among the living any longer. She abbreviates her day "back home" with this lament for the blindness with which people stumble through life without ever noticing how sacred life's ordinary moments really are:

> So all that was going on, and we never noticed. Take me back up the hill to my grave. But first: Wait! One more look. Goodbye, goodbye world. Goodbye, Grover's Corners. . . . Goodbye to clocks ticking . . . and Mama's sunflowers. And food and coffee. And new-ironed dresses and hot baths . . . and sleeping and waking up. Oh, earth, you're too wonderful for anybody to realize you.[18]

Then Emily gathers up the whole speech in a single, final, unforgettable question: "Do any human beings ever realize life while they live it?"

Now that Emily was seeing life from the perspective of one who had died, she knew how sacred was an ordinary moment, how precious was a single day. As long as she was alive, she had never "noticed"; she had never fully "realized life while she was living it." Now she couldn't understand how people could miss so much, could fail to notice the beauty of every ordinary day.

The only way we ever begin fully to realize life while we are living it is to see life for the precious, passing limited gift it is. We are going to die someday. Unless we are living in the generation that will witness the return of Christ and the end of the age, we will all die. That means that someday is going to be the last day. To embrace that truth is not to be paralyzed by living our lives in the shadow of our own death. Rather, to embrace the truth that someday is going to be the last day is to be energized by living our lives in the light of our own death. Looking at life in the light of death helps us to "stay caught up" with our family and our friends. To look at life in the light of death is to see life as the sacred gift from God that it really is, every day.

Someday is going to be the last day. Someday, we will die. Our own death will bring us, by God's grace, into God's nearer presence, where life finally will be unhindered, uninterrupted, unbounded, and free. That is our sacred, enduring, and abiding hope. It is the hope made real for us in the resurrection of Christ our Lord. Someday will be the last day, but that someday will also be the first day. In ways that transcend anything that any of us can even begin to imagine, our last day will be our first day in God's unhindered presence. Until that day, we will stay most fully alive by living each day in the light of our own death. Amen.

LIFE, IN THE LIGHT OF DEATH

What is your life?
For you are a mist
that appears for a little while
and then vanishes.
— *James 4:14b*

By a departing light
We see acuter quite
Than by a wick that stays.
There's something in the flight
That clarifies the sight
And decks the rays.
— *Emily Dickinson*

When Families Say Goodbye

All the hellos I have ever met have had something in common. They have all been carrying something out of sight. The something that is hidden behind every hello is a goodbye. Every hello that has ever been spoken has had a goodbye tucked away somewhere, deep inside, waiting for some moving day or some graduation day or some retiring or relocating or dying day, some eventual, inevitable someday when the goodbye that was hidden in the hello will find its way out into the open.

That is just the unalterable, inescapable nature of life. In the entire history of the world, there has never once been a hello that wasn't carrying a goodbye in its back pocket. And the more that first hello turns out to matter, the more that last goodbye turns out to hurt. Such is the way of life. The only way to escape having someday to say a goodbye that really hurts is to avoid ever saying a hello that really matters. But never to say a hello that really matters means never to know the immense joy of loving your family or of having real friends. You cannot anesthetize yourself to the eventual pain of a goodbye that hurts without also numbing yourself to the incredible joy of a hello that matters.

John Claypool, in a wonderful sermon called "Choose Your Pain," offers the insightful observation that our choice in life is not whether we will have some pain or no pain, but only what kind of pain we will have.[19] The option of "no pain" is simply not an option. We will either know the pain of loneliness and isolation, or we will know the pain of eventually having to say goodbye to a family member or a friend whom we love more than life itself. In other words, we cannot anesthetize ourselves to the pain of saying a goodbye that hurts without also numbing ourselves to the joy of saying a hello that matters.

We mustn't steel ourselves against the pain of goodbye by keeping all of our hellos shallow and loose. Families mustn't protect themselves from the pain of goodbye by such reasoning as, "We won't be living here long. Why make friends? We'll only end up saying goodbye. It isn't worth the pain." The truth that families must know is that the joy of a hello that matters is worth the pain of a goodbye that hurts.

To freely, fully love family and friends, husband or wife, mother or father, son or daughter, is, indeed, to make ourselves vulnerable to the pain of someday's eventual goodbye. The pain of goodbye is more than love's potential, possible risk; it is love's inevitable, certain price. But, even so, families just keep saying hello, though they know that the hello will someday give way to goodbye. It is better to have known the pain of standing by the edge of an open grave or waving to the back of a moving van than it is never to have known the joy of being a friend and being befriended. It is better to know the pain of saying a goodbye that hurts than never to know the joy of saying a hello that matters. Families just have to keep saying hello with joy and abandon and without steeling themselves against the risk of someday saying goodbye. To steel yourself against ever having to say a goodbye that hurts is to steal yourself, to rob your joy, and to diminish your life.

The pain of a goodbye that hurts and the joy of a hello that matters . . . Families cannot anesthetize themselves to one without numbing themselves to the other. We just have to go ahead and say the hellos that God places before us, knowing that the more the hello turns out to matter, the more the goodbye will turn out to hurt, but knowing that the God who gave us the gift of one day saying hello will give us the grace to someday say goodbye. Amen.

For everything there is a season,
and a time for every matter under heaven:
a time to be born, and a time to die.
—Ecclesiastes 3:1-2 (RSV)

Who You Are
Is Who You Were

Every now and then, in moments as unbidden as February's first jonquil and as fleeting as November's last leaf, you are, again, the child you were. It is more than just remembering something from your childhood. It is more than just a little *déjà vu*. It is more than just longing "to be a kid again." It is a moment of recognition, a moment in which you realize that who you are right now really is who you were back then.

It doesn't happen often. And you can't make it happen, so it is futile to try and "work it up." It just comes. Only seldom does it visit. Never long does it linger. But every now and then, in moments as unbidden as a rainbow's bend and as fleeting as a lightning bug's blink, it dawns on you that, no matter how all grown-up you may be, you are yet the child you were. It is a moment of recognition . . . a little shimmer of light that shows you for a second who you really are. Who you are is who you were.

It is a moment of recognition that travels mostly on the quiet wings of simple things. I have never been able to conjure it up, but it has conjured up on me all by itself in some unplanned moments at some unlikely places. A couple of times, that moment of recognition has so utterly seized me that it left me immobilized by the presence of God . . . a sacramental moment in which I knew that however much I had changed, I was yet, somehow, the child I once was.

It happened once in the garden plot behind the house where I grew up. I was thirty-eight years old. The rest of the family was in the house. I wandered away from the others, across the back yard, past the tool shed, through the rickety gate, beyond the hog-wire fence, into the sandy soil of the garden that my now aged and dying father had plowed forever but would never plow again. As I stood there, alone, in the cold wind of a December sunset, I glanced down at my shiny black shoes, dusty gray from my journey to the center of the field. And it happened. As unbidden as the firewood spark that leaps out into the parlor, and as fleeting as the chimney smoke that grays off into the cloud, it came and went. It was a moment in which I knew that the man in the black wing tips, standing in the garden, hoping against hope that his father would soon go back to plowing, was the same person as the kid in the black high-tops, working in the garden, hoping against hope that his daddy would soon stop plowing. I knew, for one silent moment, that who I am is who I was. I don't just remember things from that kid's life; I am that kid. And I knew it. For a powerful, sacred moment I understood that who I am *now* is, in some inexplicable but undeniable way, who I was *then*.

It happened again the night he died. As I stood with my hand on my father's forehead and watched the heart monitor's rough places become plain, it happened again. For a moment, for one agonizingly sad, unspeakably sacred moment, it dawned on me that I was just a kid whose father was gone. It came and went in a breath. It didn't last as long as the wink of a dove's eye. I believe it comes to most grown-ups when one of their parents dies. It is a sad but sacred moment, when, for one unbidden, fleeting, thin splinter of a second, it occurs to you that you're just a kid who no longer has a mama or a daddy. For one sacred moment, you recognize yourself, and you know that who you are is who you were. You don't just remember that child you used to be. You *are* that child you used to be.

Needless to say, you have to be careful with all of this talk about "who you are is who you were." The other side of the truth is that "who you are is who you have become." In many ways, who you are is not at all who you were. In fact, in most ways, who you are is who you have become. We have changed in a long list of ways since we were children. We don't look the same or think the same or act the same. Who we now are is quite different from who we once were. We are not the same because we have aged physically. We are not the same because we have matured emotionally. We are not the same because we have trusted God's grace and been converted to a new life ("So if anyone is in Christ, there is a new creation: everything old has passed away; see, everything has become new" [2 Cor 5:17]). We are not the same because we have grown theologically ("But grow in the grace and knowledge of our Lord and Savior Jesus Christ" [2 Pet 3:18a]). We are not the same because we are all grown-up ("When I was a child, I spoke like a child, I thought like a child, I reasoned like a child; when I became an adult, I put an end to childish ways" [1 Cor 13:11]).

And yet, there are those moments, those quiet, sacred, unbidden, fleeting moments when you realize that somewhere deep down inside of you is that little girl. Somewhere at the hidden center of you is that little boy. You will probably know it best when one of your parents dies . . . and in a tiny handful of other unbidden, fleeting moments that are scattered throughout a lifetime.

It is not a "second childhood." It is the first childhood, sneaking up on us, catching up to us from behind, saying in a whisper, "You're it." And then it is gone, but it leaves us knowing that, no matter how grown-up we are, no matter how much we have changed, who we are is, somehow, who we were. (Of course, we dare not say anything about it. It just wouldn't do to mention it. No one would understand.) But though no one would understand what you said, everyone would know what you meant. Because, for everyone, it is somehow true. Who we are is who we were. Amen.

*Truly I tell you,
whoever does not receive
the kingdom of God as a little child
will never enter it.*

—*Luke 18:17*

Who's That on Your Refrigerator?

"Who's that on your refrigerator?" At first glance it seems a strange question, one that conjures up vague images of visitors lounging around on the top of your freezer . . . strangers chilling on your frost-free Kenmore . . . guests cooling their heels with their feet propped up on your icemaker. "Who's that on your refrigerator?" What kind of question is that?

At first glance it does seem a little strange. But at second glance, "Who's that on your refrigerator?" doesn't look nearly so odd. In fact, now that I think about it, I can actually remember literally being asked, "Who's that on your refrigerator?" The question was raised, not because we have ever had anybody reclining on our refrigerator's roof, but because we have always had somebody clinging to our refrigerator door. Or, to be more specific, we have always had someone's picture clinging to our refrigerator door. There are always a few pictures of family and friends holding on for dear life to the door of our refrigerator. They stay up there, in the right place, by the mysterious tug of some little magnets that won't let them go, but they got up there, in the first place, by the mysterious tug of some other powers that won't let us go, the gentle powers of memory, love, family, and friendship that keep us holding on for dear life to the people who are up there on our refrigerator.

Someone has to hold a very significant place in your life in order for them to have a spot on your refrigerator. You may have dozens of photographs in boxes, books, closets, and corners, but you only have a few on your refrigerator. Whenever I go into a kitchen, my eyes eventually end up reading the pictures on the refrigerator door. In fact, I have even asked, a time or two, that strange question, "Who's that on your refrigerator?" Usually the answer reveals that, while it may be a banana-shaped magnet that keeps the picture up there in the right place, it was a heart-shaped tug that put the picture up there in the first place. People don't put casual acquaintances on their refrigerator. No. Those are mostly reserved seats, held for people who were in your heart long before they were on your refrigerator.

In fact, if you really want to know a family, ask them who those people are up there on their refrigerator. You will probably learn a lot about the friendships that mean the most to them, those rare but wonderful friendships that fit inside the frame of that beautiful old verse from Proverbs, "There is a friend who sticks closer than kin." Those are the friends who make it to the refrigerator door, the ones who stick closer even than a brother or sister.

Every family needs a few of those friends. No family has a lot of them, but every family needs a few of them. Families need friends. A family can survive without friends, but families are healthiest and happiest when some of the air they breathe comes from outside their own home. Family was not created to meet every single human need. Family was not designed to function in isolation like a self-sufficient, free-standing, disconnected island. No family, however devoted, loving, and strong, can meet every need of its members. That simply was never the intention for family. Families need to breathe from a larger air. Families need to invest time and energy and money in people outside their own walls. Families need friends. A tiny handful of those friends may even turn out to be the kind that end up on your refrigerator. You know, the kind whose picture can only be captured inside that ancient, beautiful frame: "There is a friend who sticks closer than kin."

Those kinds of friends are rare. No family has a roomful of them. But every family needs a handful, or at least a heartful, of them. The famous twentieth-century American poet, Dan Seals, described them with those wonderful words from his beautiful ballad, "One Friend."

> I always thought you were the best,
> I guess I always will.
> I always felt that we were blessed,
> And I feel that way still.
> Sometimes we took the hard road,
> But we always saw it through.
> If I had only one friend left,
> I'd want it to be you.

> Someone who understands me,
> And knows me inside out.
> And helps keep me together,
> And believes without a doubt,
> That I could move a mountain.
> Someone to tell it to.
> If I had only one friend left,
> I'd want it to be you.[20]

Those kinds of friends are the ones whose snapshots get mixed in with the family photos on the refrigerator door. Every family needs some of those kinds of friends. Needing friends doesn't mean that your family is deficient. To the contrary, the healthiest families are those families that gladly recognize their need to breathe the larger air of friendship. Along the way, a few times in a lifetime, you may be so graced by God as to have a friend who loves "at all times." That kind of friendship is a gift from God, a gift of grace that even the healthiest of families will always need. Amen.

> *A friend loves at all times.*
> —*Proverbs 17:17*

> *Some friends play at friendship,*
> *but a true friend sticks closer*
> *than one's nearest kin.*
> —*Proverbs 18:24*

How Does Christmas Feel?

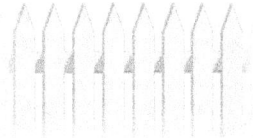

When I was a high school student, I did not compile a particularly enviable record as an athlete or as a scholar. I did, however, achieve a fleeting measure of notoriety as an Elvis impersonator. This otherwise useless talent gained me a lofty, though transient, place of preeminence among my peers, whom I would frequently entertain in the lunch line with a bar or two from that grammatically flawed but sensitive ballad, "You Ain't Nothing But a Hound Dog."

The Elvis business, as one might suspect, was especially brisk at Christmastime. My yuletide Elvis repertoire included a dizzily upbeat, but nonetheless moving, rendition of Brenda Lee's "Rockin' Around the Christmas Tree," which I sang in Elvis' voice, with background accompaniment provided by an 8-track tape, featuring those paragons of holiday harmony, Alvin and the Chipmunks. The finale of those holiday concerts was, needless to say, that perennial classic, "Blue Christmas." But my personal favorite was a more introspective, misty-eyed number called "Why Can't Every Day Be Like Christmas?" The lyrics have faded to a dim memory since I lost my leather jacket and shaved my sideburns, but, if I remember correctly, the refrain goes something like this:

> Why can't every day be like Christmas?
> Why can't that feeling go on endlessly?
> For if every day could be just like Christmas,
> What a wonderful world this would be.

A wonderful world it would be, indeed, if every day could be just like Christmas. But, despite Elvis' wistful inquiry into the possibilities of such an idyllic arrangement, alas, it cannot be. Every day just cannot be like Christmas. We cannot skip school, miss mail, and sip cider every day. Every day cannot be like Christmas. It just wouldn't work. However, though every other day is not like Christmas, there is a sense in which Christmas is like every other day. Although every other day is not like Christmas, Christmas is like every other day, only more so. At Christmastime we feel the same emotions we feel the rest of the year, only we feel those emotions more deeply and fully at Christmas. There really is something different about Christmas. But the something different is not that we feel new feelings at Christmas. Rather, it is that we feel familiar old feelings more deeply and fully at Christmastime than at other times. It is in that sense that Christmas feels like every other day, only more so.

If we are inclined to be generous every day, we will feel even more generous at Christmas. If we enjoy children all the time, we will enjoy them even more at Christmastime. If we work to help homeless persons throughout the year, we will help even more at Christmas. If we are always concerned for those who are hungry, we will be even more concerned at Christmastime. If spending time with our friends is important to us all year long, then time spent with friends will be even more important to us at Christmas. If we are moved by beautiful music at other times, we will be more deeply moved at Christmastime. If we are far away from a home that we remember and miss on other days, then we will remember home more clearly and miss home more dearly on Christmas day. If we feel, at other times, the absence of a parent, spouse, or child who has died, then the pain of their absence will grow deeper as Christmas day grows nearer. If, on other days, we rejoice to know that God has come to us in the life of Jesus, then we will rejoice all the more at Christmas.

It is true. Though every other day is not like Christmas, Christmas is like every other day, only more so. The highest joys and deepest pains and finest commitments and dearest affections we feel at other times are the same joys, pains, commitments, and affections we feel at Christmastime; only at Christmastime we feel them more so. In gladness and in sorrow, Christmas feels about like most other days, only more so.

That truth is nowhere more beautifully captured than in the first of the "Christmas sections" of Alfred Tennyson's "In Memoriam." Writing about the very first Christmas after Arthur Hallam's untimely death had devastated Tennyson and his family, Tennyson wrote that he was so sad that it would have suited him if he had died before Christmas came, but, once he heard the bells of Christmas, he felt again a joy he could not resist alongside the grief he could not escape.

> The time draws near the birth of Christ.
>   The moon is hid, the night is still;
> The Christmas bells from hill to hill
>   Answer each other in the mist.
>
> This year I slept and woke with pain,
>   I almost wished no more to wake,
> And prayed my hold on life would break
>   Before I heard those bells again.
>
> But the bells my troubled spirit rule,
>   For they controlled me when a boy;
> They bring me sorrow touched with joy,
>   The merry, merry bells of Yule.[21]

Tennyson said that the bells of Christmas would not leave him alone. He had decided to be sad and miss Christmas. He had decided to be unmoved by the sights and sounds of Christmas. But he found, to his surprise, that those Christmas bells that so magnificently controlled him when he was a boy were still able to wield a little power over his life, and, though they could not ring away his sadness, those bells did, at least, leave him with his sorrow touched by joy. Tennyson found his sackcloth hemmed in tinsel. The dirge he chanted was joined by a carol. The pall he bore was trimmed with garland. At Christmastime, his sorrow was touched by joy. He felt no new feeling at Christmas. Rather, he felt the familiar old feelings of sorrow and joy, only he felt them more than he had felt them before.

Which is almost always the way Christmas feels. Christmas feels a lot like every other day, only more so. Families set themselves up for an annual disappointment when they expect to feel something altogether new and completely different at Christmas. What we should expect, instead, is to feel things old and familiar, but to feel those old and familiar emotions and memories, pains and joys, commitments and affections all the more deeply, powerfully, beautifully, and completely. Because that is how Christmas feels . . . a lot like every other day, only a whole lot more! Amen.

But the angel said to them,
"Do not be afraid; for see—
I am bringing you good news
of great joy for all the people:
to you is born this day
in the city of David a Savior,
who is the Messiah, the Lord."
—Luke 2:10-11

The mystery of Christmas filled our hearts.
We understood little, but we sensed a great deal.
—Ferrol Sams, *Christmas Gift*

So Take a Lot of Pictures

Ferrol Sams, in his beautiful book *Christmas Gift*, framed the lingering power of a remembered place in his unforgettable observation that "happiness is not a place, but in memory it is frequently identified with one."[22] Truer words have never been spoken. It is a fact that happiness is not a place. But it is also a fact that, in memory, happiness is almost always associated with a place.

I have long known that was so, but I never knew it in its full power until I leaned one day against a familiar old, but recently sold, fence. It was a hog-wire fence, five feet high, held more or less upright by some old weather-beaten, half-rotten creosote posts. Thirty years ago, I helped my father dig the holes in which those posts still wobble. I helped him string the wire against which those posts still lean. That fence had been my fence for as long as it had been in the world. But the time came when it was wisest and best, for everyone, to sell the fence. It was the right thing to do. The children were grown and gone. The chapters had turned. Life had changed. So the fence and all its wiry arms embraced were sold. The big yard and the small house inside the fence became someone else's place.

I will never forget the first time I drove up to the place and realized it was no longer mine. I parked across the road, walked through the churchyard next door, and found myself leaning against the fence that now belonged to someone new. I gazed over the top row of rusty old rectangles at the yard that was once my place. I could never remember a day when that yard was not mine to rule and conquer, but now I was outside, staring at it from behind a fence post that my little boy hands had long ago left leaning crooked but standing proud. I felt like a stranger, yet I was just outside the gate of the one place in the world that I knew best.

Just a few feet from where I stood was my old plywood backboard, its wobbly, netless rim barely holding on (through which I often sank, at the buzzer, the winning shot in the NCAA finals). Over to the left was the rosebush (where, on numerous occasions, I had scored the winning touchdown in the Rose Bowl). Back near the junkhouse was the clothesline pole (where I frequently saved my mama from a grizzly bear so she could finish hanging out the sheets). And up by the house was the pine stump (which I had often ascended, in humble gratitude, to receive the Heisman Trophy, the National League M.V.P. Award, and any number of Olympic gold medals).

This was home, the yard inside the fence, the place where, every Easter, my sister had found the elusive

Prize Egg, and where, every Christmas, my father had muttered harsh words at the uncooperative Tree Stand. This was my world. I had worked there and wept there. I had laughed there and played there. I had lived there and loved there. And now, it was no longer mine. I had lost my place.

It happens. It will probably happen to you. In the unfolding of life, it will happen because it must happen. If you live long enough, you will probably, someday, lose your place. It is eventually necessary, and it is usually right. The pain of it does not diminish the rightness of it. And the rightness of it does not diminish the pain of it. Families eventually, inevitably, lose their place.

Of course, in our most mature moments, we all know that happiness, after all, is not a place. But we also know that, while happiness is not a place, in memory it is almost always associated with a place.

Sooner or later, if your family is like most families, you will leave an old place to go live in a new place. The first time you go back by the old place and you can't go in, it will feel for all the world as though you've lost your place.

So take a lot of pictures. Because someday, you will probably lose your place. And you will wish you could go back in and look around, just one more time. So . . . take a lot of pictures. Amen.

How could we sing the Lord's song
in a foreign land?
—*Psalm 137:4*

Tears, idle tears, I know not what they mean,
Tears from the depth of some divine despair
Rise in the heart, and gather to the eyes,
In looking on the happy autumn-fields,
And thinking of the days that are no more.
                            —Alfred Tennyson

The Tug of Home

Several months after we moved to a new and distant place, Marcia received a beautiful gift from a dear friend. It is a framed painting of a little house out in the country—tin roof, stone wall, rock chimney, yard flowers. Inscribed across the bottom of the picture are these tender and insightful words:

> You never really leave a place you love.
> You take part of it with you,
> And you leave part of you behind.

I have no idea who first wrote those words. But I know someone who could have written them. The same person who wrote the 137th Psalm could just as easily have written the words in the picture, because the words in the picture are a framed echo of the words in the psalm. "You never really leave a place you love. You take part of it with you, and you leave part of you behind." That is the truth that is wrapped like a clinging vine around the homesick words of Psalm 137.

Psalm 137 was a song of the exiled children of God who had been carried away captive from their homeland. They had been removed from their home place by Nebuchadnezzar's army. They had been carried away to the strange and distant land of Babylon, and there they would be for a long, long time.

So they wrote a song. It was the blues! The first line said, "We sat down and cried when we remembered home." It was a ballad about being displaced. It was an anthem about being removed from the home that was once all around them but was now far behind them. That song made it into the Bible as Psalm 137. It uncovers the pain of displacement and the tug of home when it wonders out loud, "How can we sing the Lord's song in a strange land? Babylon may be where we live, but it is not our home."

I think that most folks can understand that psalm. Because, for many, many people, there is a home that sometimes tugs from behind. You never really leave a place like that. You really do take part of it with you. And you really do leave part of you behind.

I suppose that is why I have a Yoo-Hoo chocolate drink bottle in the top drawer of my desk at home. It isn't just your ordinary, everyday, run-of-the-mill Yoo-Hoo chocolate drink bottle. It is a very special bottle, because it is full of very special dirt . . . dirt that I dug up and bottled in the final weeks before we moved to Washington. There is a spoonful of dirt from our yard where Joshua and Maria played for nine years. There is a spoonful of dirt (which I retrieved under cover of darkness) from behind home plate at the field where Josh was the catcher on a championship baseball team. There is a spoonful of dirt from Edward and Marcia Howell's farm in Cochran, Georgia, one of our favorite fishing holes. There is a spoonful from the old garden plot where my father used to plow and my mother used to pick, and a small scoop I harvested from the top of Daddy's grave on the last stop we made as we were leaving town. Every now and then, I pull out the Yoo-Hoo bottle and shake that dirt around. I look at it real hard. Sometimes, I even take off the top and smell the past that is planted in that soil.

So, I understand Psalm 137. And so do you. Because you, too, have some place, back there somewhere, that tugs at your heart every now and then. Thomas Wolfe told the truth when he said that you can't go home again. He was right; no one ever really "goes back home." But the other side of that truth is that no one ever fully leaves home either. You take part of it with you. You leave part of yourself behind. Home tugs. And sometimes, the tug of home comes from behind.

But not always. Sometimes, the tug of home comes from beyond, because we not only have a home that is way back behind us; we also have a home that is far out beyond us. It is the home to which the writer of the Revelation pointed when he talked about a place where there would be no more sorrow or pain or tears or death, a place where there would be no more anything to fear or dread, a place where God would be at home with people and people would be at home with God. That is the home that is out there, beyond us. One of these days, somehow, somewhere, someway, someday, the kingdoms of this world will be swallowed up into the Kingdom of God's goodness and grace, and we will be at home with God.

That is not starry-eyed optimism. That is not misty-eyed sentimentality. That is clear-eyed realism and wide-eyed hope. It rings true to even the most jaded, calloused, and skeptical ears. Somewhere, somehow, someway, someday, we will be at home with God, and God will be at home with us. It is out there beyond us. It will finally be home.

We have a home, way back behind us. And we have a home, far out beyond us. And we have a home, deep down inside us. Way down inside us, at the deep down center of who we are, there is the home we finally, fully come to when we finally, fully trust ourselves to God's grace.

That, it seems to me, is the truth that is tucked away in that wonderful story we call the parable of the prodigal son. On the surface of the story, a weary, hungry, embarrassed boy is coming to the home that was tugging at him from behind. But, at another level, the story is a parable, not only about that boy's homecoming, but about you and me and a home that tugs at us all from way down deep inside, at the center of our soul.

Sooner or later, you and I must come home to the truth that is truer than all the other truth in the world, the truth that God loves us, not for what we do or what we achieve or what we accomplish, but just because we are the objects of God's enduring, abiding, unconditional love. There is, of course, a word for that kind of love. The word is "grace."

Grace is what the boy in the story found when he "came to himself" and came home. When he "came to himself," he said, "Wait a minute. This is not me. I'm going to go home. I don't know if they will still have me, but I'm going back home because this just isn't me." So he limped back home with his pocket empty, his head down, and his speech rehearsed. But before he could even get out the first paragraph, he was embraced in his father's arms of love. When the boy came to himself, he turned toward home. When he got home, he found grace waiting to receive him. And then, at last, he was truly, finally home.

There is a home, deep down inside of you and me. It is a quiet, peaceful, restful, joyful center. We find that quiet home, deep down inside, when we "come to ourselves" and get in touch with the ultimate reality of life—the reality that we are the objects of God's enduring, abiding, saving, embracing grace.

Until you believe that, you will never find the quiet, restful home that is deep within you. Because until you finally, fully, abandon yourself to God's grace and trust yourself to God's grace and believe that God's grace is for you, then you will never be able to rest. You will always wonder if you've done enough or given enough to get on God's good side. You will always wonder if you have been righteous enough or busy enough to gain God's favor.

Until you come home to grace, you never know whether or not you have been good enough to gain God's love. The not knowing leaves you forever unsettled and insecure. That kind of endless insecurity will eventually turn you into a bitter, angry, demanding kind of person, because, until you have received grace for yourself, you cannot give grace to others. The truth is, until you just finally "come to yourself" and realize that you are a child of God's grace, you will always be at war with yourself. And, as Fred Craddock has so wisely observed, when we are at war with ourselves, we make casualties out of everyone around us, especially those who are closest to us.[23] But we don't have to live that way. We can be changed. We can be saved from all that by trusting ourselves to, and casting ourselves upon, God's grace.

When we finally hear the gospel of God's grace and trust it and believe it and give ourselves to it, then life is changed. We are more quiet and kind. We no longer feel the need to have the last word or win the next argument. We still have our problems, worries, complexities, fears, and flaws, but at the center of our soul there is a quiet, restful, settled place, a quiet place from which we say our words and live our lives. We are, somehow, already home, at home with ourselves, and at home with God. And it is then that we discover what Jesus meant when he talked about "being born again." We really do have a whole new life. We are, at last, at home—at home with ourselves and at home with God.

When I was a boy back home, we frequently traveled to Kite, Georgia, on Saturday afternoons. Kite was where my father's parents, Eugene and Bessie Poole, lived. Pretty much the same thing happened every time we arrived at my grandparents' home. Ma Bessie would feed us fried chicken. Then, about sundown, Daddy

Gene would let me help him carry his big wooden radio out into the front yard. (He set it up on a table out in the yard because he was seeking a faraway station from a distant port-of-call, and the reception was always better outside.) We would unroll the extension cords, stick a straightened-out coat hanger in the top of the broken-off radio antenna, wrap the coat hanger in tin foil, and, then, with all our technology firmly in place, we would, with breathless anticipation, turn the dial to A.M. 650. Wonder of wonders, it would always come through . . . all the way from Nashville, Tennessee, brought to you live by those nice folks that make Goo-Goo Clusters. It was the Grand Ole Opry.

Now, my grandmother took a rather dim view of such worldly proceedings. So, invariably, in a little while, much too soon to suit me, she would snatch me from the perilous clutches of Merle Haggard and Loretta Lynn by calling me into the house and sitting me down by her on the piano bench, where she would retrieve my wayward soul by singing hymns to me. Her repertoire included "Amazing Grace," "Standing on the Promises," and "What a Friend We Have in Jesus." But the one that always tugged strongest at my heart was a more plaintive and haunting piece. I knew every word of it by memory, but I never grew tired of it or cold to it. The chorus went like this:

> Coming home,
> Coming home,
> Never more to roam,
> Open wide thine arms of love,
> Lord, I'm coming home.

Oh, how those words used to tug, and how they yet tug, at my heart. It feels like the tug of home . . . the tug of the home that is way back behind us, the tug of the home that is far out beyond us, and the tug of the home that is deep down inside us.

It is never too late to come home when God is holding the door. God loves you. If you will cast yourself upon that truth, you can be at home with God, and even with yourself. You can find a quiet home, somewhere deep down inside. It is a home you can take with you, no matter where you go. Even if you have to leave your old home, you can carry this home wherever you go. And it can carry you.

Home does tug. From way back behind us, from far out beyond us, and from deep down inside us, home does tug. Thanks be to God for the tug of home. Amen.

By the rivers of Babylon—
there we sat down and there we wept
when we remembered Zion.
—*Psalm 137:1*

But when he came to himself he said. . . . I will get up and go to my father. . . . But while he was still far off, his father saw him and was filled with compassion; he ran and put his arms around him and kissed him.
—*Luke 15:17-20*

*And I heard a loud voice from the throne saying,
"See the home of God is among mortals."*
—Revelation 21:3a

Epilogue

The Picture Spills Over the Frame

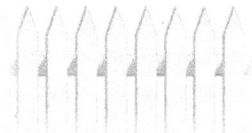

I am writing these words while sitting on a bench at the National Gallery of Art in Washington, D.C. I have wandered through the entire building, and, while I am not the most observant student who ever pondered a painting, I have, nonetheless, been able to surmise that every picture in this building fits inside its frame. All these pictures seem to have made peace with their frames. None of them are spilling over the edges. There are just worlds and worlds of pictures here in the National Gallery. As far as I can tell, they all fit inside their frames.

So it is when life is still. When life is captured still by a brush and a stroke, or a film and a flash, you can put it inside a frame, and it will stay there. But not so when life is being lived. When life is living, changing, growing, deciding, moving, stumbling, birthing, playing, working, laughing, crying, and dying, it tends to spill over the edges of the settled, defined frames in which we try to capture it. Life, when it is actually being lived, is not nearly so neat and manageable as it looks in frameable pictures.

Several years ago, Baptist theologian Richard Wilson and I were reflecting on the death of a bright young friend of ours when Dr. Wilson said, "I just can't make this picture fit inside the frame." Then, sometime later, a similar image fell across my path when I read a passage from Frederick Buechner in which he spoke of the parables of Jesus as being so simultaneously simple and complicated, sad and joyous, that they cannot be reduced to simple slogans that can be "framed on the living room wall." The parables, Buechner suggested, are so alive and living and moving that they are "not suitable for framing."[24]

Those images from Richard Wilson and Frederick Buechner helped me to give a name to a nameless feeling I've long had, the hard-to-describe feeling that you can't ever quite put a frame around the family picture while it is living. The living family portrait won't fit inside a frame. It isn't simple enough or manageable enough to corral inside a frame. It will always spill over the frame. It is a picture about birthing and dying. It is about baby showers and graduations and retirement dinners and funerals. The family portrait is about complex decisions and uncertain moments. It is about worship and work and rest and play. It happens in waiting rooms and dining rooms and emergency rooms. The family photo is about everything from the Little League double with two outs in the sixth inning, to the talent show debut on the stage of the school cafetorium, to the trip downtown for more chemotherapy, to the decision about which nursing home seems to be the best for father.

The family photo only fits inside a frame when you get everybody in front of the fireplace ("Squeeze in a little tighter. Okay now . . . Everybody ready? Keep your eyes open this time. On three: One, two . . .") and snap a flash. But when life is actually being lived, the family portrait always spills over the edges of the frame, because when life is being lived, there is ambiguity that can't be simplified, complexity that can't be resolved, and grief that can't be abbreviated. There are decisions that must be made about staying or moving. There are the twin, but opposite, realities of holding on and letting go, of wanting to do more and needing to do less, of never being able to "go back home," yet never quite leaving home's memory and influence behind.

There are aging parents and growing children, and adults in the middle years who wish they could give more time in both directions. There is the laughter you laugh until you cry, and there is the weeping you weep until, again, you laugh. And then, there are those tears that can't be caught inside a definition; tears that defy our common categories of "tears of sorrow and tears of joy," the strange, unbidden, awkward, unexpected kind of tears that you weep when you see your closest friends approaching you in the line at the funeral home visitation. (You've been there. Or someday you will be. The deeper joy you feel at the sight of your friend opens you up to the deepest pain you feel at the death of your parent, and you embarrass yourself with tears of . . . of what? Of joy? Of sorrow? Those tears will not fit inside either frame. They suggest that our division of labor among tears may well be artificial. Perhaps there are no tears of joy or tears of sorrow. Perhaps there are just tears, all of which rise from the same deep place.)

So much of the life we live in families defies definition or explanation. The family portrait spills over the frame. There are no "how-to" videos that can resolve all the ambiguities or manage all the uncertainties. There is help to be had from books and seminars and parenting classes and such. The help is welcome and needed. But finally, the family picture cannot be reduced to a neat frame, because life keeps happening, unfolding, changing, and growing.

We will never be able to frame the living, moving family picture. But, though we cannot frame it, we can color it. We can color the family portrait in quiet, strong, and beautiful ways. We can do that by listening to the people in our families, really listening to them when they want to tell us something, listening to them until they have been heard and understood. We can help color the family picture, not only by listening to the people in our families, but also by talking to the people in our families, telling them our hopes and fears and dreams, and "saying the blessing" to them, out loud, so that they can carry into the world a deep-down, unshakable certainty that they are believed in and loved. And we can also help color the family picture in strong and beautiful ways by becoming better. We do that, at the most foundational, fundamental level, when we begin to live what our Quaker friends call "a centered life."

The centered life is a life that is colored by a quiet spirit of prayer and devotion, because it is a life that is punctuated by silent times of prayer and devotion. Over and over, the Gospels record that Jesus rose before day to pray, or slipped away to be alone, or spent the night praying to God. One reason our Lord Jesus' life was so thoroughly colored by a constant spirit of prayer is that his life was so frequently punctuated by hidden times of prayer. We are called to the same kind of life. And when we actually live that kind of life, when we really do punctuate our days with times of prayer, silence, and devotion, then our days really do become colored by a quiet spirit of prayer that makes us more gentle, more patient, and more discerning with the people in our family.

All of this is not to suggest that a daily time of devotion is a magic wand that scatters sweetness and light throughout the house. Nor do I mean to suggest that we can spend a little time in prayer in the morning and then cruise through the rest of the day on auto-pilot. None of that is true. However, the fact is, when we open our lives to God's presence in stillness, silence, prayer, and devotion, we are changed. Our lives become softened, strengthened, and colored by the spirit of Christ. We become better people. We become more patient and less angry. We cease to look on disagreements as battles that must be won or lost, so we become liberated from the need to "have the last word." We become people of quiet piety who have a keen ability to discern the difference between what matters and what doesn't. Thus, we develop a new capacity to feel intensity about the right things, which frees us to be relaxed about other things. Our family can sense a difference in us. Things that once frustrated us now amuse us. Things that once caused us to frown and fuss now cause us to smile and chuckle. This is true piety, at work in the simplest matters of life. We become more patient, more kind, more committed to the gospel, more sensitive to God, and more devoted to people. At the same time, we become more relaxed about life.

This is not a cool nonchalance, nor is it a syrupy-sweet, self-conscious façade of religion. To the contrary, this is the genuine, authentic, bone-deep piety that enables us to become fully human (in the biblical sense of the word "human," which in the beginning meant to live life in the image of God). Our lives, punctuated by times of prayer and devotion, become less fragmented and more centered. Our lives begin to reflect more of the spirit of our Lord Jesus. Our lives become colored by a quiet spirit of prayer and devotion that bends the contours of our lives to the shape of the gospel. We are changed. And our family can sense it. The family picture is colored in happier, quieter shades and hues.

The family portrait cannot be framed while it is developing. Life is too unmanageable to fit inside a frame. There is too much ambiguity and uncertainty, too much letting go and going on, too much joy and sorrow to capture the developing family portrait inside a frame. But if the family picture cannot be framed, at least it can be colored. It can be colored in wonderful ways when we listen to one another and talk to one another, and when we listen to God and talk to God so silently, openly, and regularly that our lives become centered and softened and strengthened and colored by the God who loves us, the God of grace, the God who is, ultimately, our true and lasting Home. Amen.

Notes

[1] Jimmy Carter, *Living Faith* (New York: Times Books, 1996) 263.

[2] For this perspective on "the blessing," I am indebted to Scott Walker, *The Freedom Factor* (San Francisco: Harper & Row, 1989) 2-21.

[3] Richard Leigh and Layng Martine, Jr., "The Greatest Man I Never Knew," from Reba McEntire's *Greatest Hits Volume Two* (MCA Records, Inc.).

[4] Burton Banks Collins and Karen Taylor Good, "How Can I Help You to Say Goodbye?" (Reynsong Publishing, Burton B. Collins Publishing, W. B. M. Music Corporation, K. T. Good Music [SESAC], 1993).

[5] Statistics secured from the Employee Relocation Council, 1720 N St. NW, Washington DC, and the American Movers Conference, 1611 Duke St., Alexandria VA.

[6] As quoted in John Claypool, *The Light Within You* (Waco TX: Word Books, 1983) 159.

[7] Frederick Buechner, *Whistling in the Dark* (New York: HarperCollins, 1993) 110.

[8] Quoted from one of Ernest Campbell's quarterly newsletters, date unknown.

[9] I heard this C. S. Lewis quote in a lecture given by John Claypool at Mercer University, Macon GA.

[10] John Claypool, *Opening Blind Eyes* (Nashville: Abingdon Press, 1983) 23.

[11] For this perspective on Adam and Eve, see John Claypool's sermon, "You Can't Have It All," in *The Twentieth-Century Pulpit*, vol. 2, James W. Cox and Patricia Parrent Cox, eds. (Nashville: Abingdon Press, 1981) 26.

[12]From a newspaper article by Erma Bombeck, date unknown.

[13]Walter B. Shurden, unpublished sermon, preached 26 January 1997, First Baptist Church, Washington DC.

[14]Raymond A. Cook, *Mountain Singer* (Atlanta: Cherokee Publishing Co., 1980) 262.

[15]William Sloane Coffin, "Alex's Death," in *A Chorus of Witnesses*, Thomas G. Long and Cornelius Plantinga, Jr., eds. (Grand Rapids: Eerdmans, 1994) 265.

[16]Walker, 53-66.

[17]Buechner, 117.

[18]Thornton Wilder, *Our Town* (New York: Harper & Row, 1938) 100.

[19]John Claypool, *God Is an Amateur* (Cincinnati OH: Forward Movement Publications, 1994) 29.

[20]Dan Seals, "One Friend," from *The Best Sound Recording* (Capitol Records, 1987).

[21]Alfred Tennyson, "In Memoriam, A.H.H.," in *Tennyson's Poetry*, Robert W. Hill, Jr., ed. (New York: W. W. Norton & Co., 1971) 134.

[22]Ferrol Sams, *Christmas Gift* (Atlanta: Longstreet Press, 1989) 4.

[23]Fred Craddock, "Praying Through Clenched Teeth," *The Twentieth-Century Pulpit*, vol. 2, James W. Cox and Patricia Parrent Cox, eds. (Nashville: Abingdon Press, 1981) 50.

[24]Frederick Buechner, *Listening to Your Life* (New York: HarperCollins, 1992) 310.

Charles E. Poole has touched thousands of lives as an author and minister. His following is increasing because of his talent for finding perfect, healing words when people need them the most. This, his third book, follows two bestselling titles, Don't Cry Past Tuesday and Is Life Fair?. Poole is currently senior minister at First Baptist Church in Washington, D.C.

He has also served churches in Georgia and North Carolina. He is a graduate of Macon College, Mercer University, and Southeastern Baptist Theological Seminary. He and his wife, Marcia, have two children, Joshua and Maria.

For as long as there have been families, families have needed a place to rest. Everywhere I look, I see weary families. Families are struggling to keep up with the demands of life, figure out the complexities of life, and live through the difficulties of life. Families are trying to keep pace with overburdened schedules and overcommitted calendars.

If a book can become, for a few moments, "a place," then, hopefully, the words inside this book can clear out a restful, quiet place where weary families can go for a little while, and be still, and remember. . . . Remember home and an old homeplace . . . Remember God's grace, which often calls us to say "yes" and do more, but sometimes invites us to say "no" and do less . . . Remember friends and children and friendship and childhood . . . Remember that life, even at its best, is only going to get so good, and that life, even at its longest, is only going to last so long . . . Remember that every family is the same when it comes to death, but that every death is not the same when it comes to families . . . Remember that, though everything has changed, everything is still the same.

That's the sort of resting and remembering place that weary families seem to need. Families need a little place, every now and then, to rest and remember and feel God's tug and know God's grace. I don't know if books can clear out a little space and make such a place. But if they can, I hope that this one will.
—Charles E. Poole

Other available titles from

Beyond the American Dream
Millard Fuller

In 1968, Millard finished the story of his journey from pauper to millionaire to home builder. His wife, Linda, occasionally would ask him about getting it published, but Millard would reply, "Not now. I'm too busy." This is that story. *978-1-57312-563-5 272 pages/pb* **$20.00**

Blissful Affliction
The Ministry and Misery of Writing
Judson Edwards

Edwards draws from more than forty years of writing experience to explore why we use the written word to change lives and how to improve the writing craft. *978-1-57312-594-9 144 pages/pb* **$15.00**

Choosing Gratitude
Learning to Love the Life You Have
James A. Autry

Autry reminds us that gratitude is a choice, a spiritual—not social—process. He suggests that if we cultivate gratitude as a way of being, we may not change the world and its ills, but we can change our response to the world. If we fill our lives with moments of gratitude, we will indeed love the life we have. *978-1-57312-614-4 144 pages/pb* **$15.00**

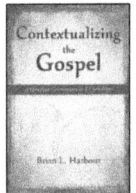
Contextualizing the Gospel
A Homiletic Commentary on 1 Corinthians
Brian L. Harbour

Harbour examines every part of Paul's letter, providing a rich resource for those who want to struggle with the difficult texts as well as the simple texts, who want to know how God's word—all of it—intersects with their lives today. *978-1-57312-589-5 240 pages/pb* **$19.00**

Dance Lessons
Moving to the Beat of God's Heart
Jeanie Miley

Miley shares her joys and struggles a she learns to "dance" with the Spirit of the Living God. *978-1-57312-622-9 240 pages/pb* **$19.00**

To order call **1-800-747-3016** or visit **www.helwys.com**

Daniel (Smyth & Helwys Annual Bible Study series)
Keeping Faith When the Heat Is On
Bill Ireland

Daniel is a book about resistance. It was written to people under pressure. In the book, we will see the efforts oppressive regimes take to undermine the faith and identity of God's people. In it, we will also see the strategies God's people employed in resisting the imposition of a foreign culture, and we will see what sustained their efforts. In that vein, the book of Daniel is powerfully relevant.

Teaching Guide 978-1-57312-647-2 144 pages/pb **$14.00**
Study Guide 978-1-57312-646-5 80 pages/pb **$6.00**

A Divine Duet
Ministry and Motherhood
Alicia Davis Porterfield, ed.

Each essay in this inspiring collection is as different as the mother-minister who wrote it, from theologians to chaplains, inner-city ministers to rural-poverty ministers, youth pastors to preachers, mothers who have adopted, birthed, and done both.

978-1-57312-676-2 146 pages/pb **$16.00**

Divorce Ministry
A Guidebook
Charles Qualls

This book shares with the reader the value of establishing a divorce recovery ministry while also offering practical insights on establishing your own unique church-affiliated program. Whether you are working individually with one divorced person or leading a large group, *Divorce Ministry: A Guidebook* provides helpful resources to guide you through the emotional and relational issues divorced people often encounter.

978-1-57312-588-8 156 pages/pb **$16.00**

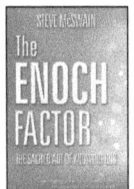

The Enoch Factor
The Sacred Art of Knowing God
Steve McSwain

The Enoch Factor is a persuasive argument for a more enlightened religious dialogue in America, one that affirms the goals of all religions—guiding followers in self-awareness, finding serenity and happiness, and discovering what the author describes as "the sacred art of knowing God."

978-1-57312-556-7 256 pages/pb **$21.00**

To order call **1-800-747-3016** or visit **www.helwys.com**

Healing Our Hurts
Coping with Difficult Emotions
Daniel Bagby

In *Healing Our Hurts*, Daniel Bagby identifies and explains all the dynamics at play in these complex emotions. Offering practical biblical insights to these feelings, he interprets faith-based responses to separate overly religious piety from true, natural human emotion. This book helps us learn how to deal with life's difficult emotions in a redemptive and responsible way.
978-1-57312-613-7 144 pages/pb **$15.00**

Hope for the Thinking Christian
Seeking a Path of Faith through Everyday Life
Stephen Reese

Readers who want to confront their faith more directly, to think it through and be open to God in an individual, authentic, spiritual encounter will find a resonant voice in Stephen Reese.
978-1-57312-553-6 160 pages/pb **$16.00**

A Hungry Soul Desperate to Taste God's Grace
Honest Prayers for Life
Charles Qualls

Part of how we *see* God is determined by how we *listen* to God. There is so much noise and movement in the world that competes with images of God. This noise would drown out God's beckoning voice and distract us. Charles Qualls's newest book offers readers prayers for that journey toward the meaning and mystery of God.
978-1-57312-648-9 152 pages/pb **$14.00**

James M. Dunn and Soul Freedom
Aaron Douglas Weaver

James Milton Dunn, over the last fifty years, has been the most aggressive Baptist proponent for religious liberty in the United States. Soul freedom—voluntary, uncoerced faith and an unfettered individual conscience before God—is the basis of his understanding of church-state separation and the historic Baptist basis of religious liberty.
978-1-57312-590-1 224 pages/pb **$18.00**

The Jesus Tribe
Following Christ in the Land of the Empire
Ronnie McBrayer

The Jesus Tribe fleshes out the implications, possibilities, contradictions, and complexities of what it means to live within the Jesus Tribe and in the shadow of the American Empire.
978-1-57312-592-5 208 pages/pb **$17.00**

To order call **1-800-747-3016** or visit **www.helwys.com**

Judaism
A Brief Guide to Faith and Practice
Sharon Pace

Sharon Pace's newest book is a sensitive and comprehensive introduction to Judaism. What is it like to be born into the Jewish community? How does belief in the One God and a universal morality shape the way in which Jews see the world? How does one find meaning in life and the courage to endure suffering? How does one mark joy and forge community ties?

978-1-57312-644-1 144 pages/pb **$16.00**

Lessons from the Cloth 2
501 More One Minute Motivators for Leaders
Bo Prosser and Charles Qualls

As the force that drives organizations to accomplishment, leadership is at a crucial point in churches, corporations, families, and almost every arena of life. Without leadership there is chaos. *With leadership there is sometimes chaos!* In this follow-up to their first volume, Bo Prosser and Charles Qualls will inspire you to keep growing in your leadership career.

978-1-57312-665-6 152 pages/pb **$11.00**

Let Me More of Their Beauty See
Reading Familiar Verses in Context
Diane G. Chen

Let Me More of Their Beauty See offers eight examples of how attention to the historical and literary settings can safeguard against taking a text out of context, bring out its transforming power in greater dimension, and help us apply Scripture appropriately in our daily lives.

978-1-57312-564-2 160 pages/pb **$17.00**

Looking Around for God
The Strangely Reverent Observations of an Unconventional Christian
James A. Autry

Looking Around for God, Autry's tenth book, is in many ways his most personal. In it he considers his unique life of faith and belief in God. Autry is a former Fortune 500 executive, author, poet, and consultant whose work has had a significant influence on leadership thinking.

978-157312-484-3 144 pages/pb **$16.00**

To order call **1-800-747-3016** or visit **www.helwys.com**

Maggie Lee for Good
Jinny and John Hinson

Maggie Lee for Good captures the essence of a young girl's boundless faith and spirit. Her parents' moving story of the accident that took her life will inspire readers who are facing loss, looking for evidence of God's sustaining grace, or searching for ways to make a meaningful difference in the lives of others.

978-1-57312-630-4 144 pages/pb **$15.00**

Making the Timeless Word Timely
A Primer for Preachers
Michael B. Brown

Michael Brown writes, "There is a simple formula for sermon preparation that creates messages that apply and engage whether your parish is rural or urban, young or old, rich or poor, five thousand members or fifty." The other part of the task, of course, involves being creative and insightful enough to know how to take the general formula for sermon preparation and make it particular in its impact on a specific congregation. Brown guides the reader through the formula and the skills to employ it with excellence and integrity.

978-1-57312-578-9 160 pages/pb **$16.00**

Meeting Jesus Today
For the Cautious, the Curious, and the Committed
Jeanie Miley

Meeting Jesus Today, ideal for both individual study and small groups, is intended to be used as a workbook. It is designed to move readers from studying the Scriptures and ideas within the chapters to recording their journey with the Living Christ.

978-1-57312-677-9 320 pages/pb **$19.00**

The Ministry Life
101 Tips for New Ministers
John Killinger

Sharing years of wisdom from more than fifty years in ministry and teaching, The Ministry Life: 101 Tips for New Ministers by John Killinger is filled with practical advice and wisdom for a minister's day-to-day tasks as well as advice on intellectual and spiritual habits to keep ministers of any age healthy and fulfilled.

978-1-57312-662-5 244 pages/pb **$19.00**

To order call **1-800-747-3016** or visit **www.helwys.com**

Mount and Mountain
Vol. 1: A Reverend and a Rabbi Talk About the Ten Commandments
Rami Shapiro and Michael Smith

Mount and Mountain represents the first half of an interfaith dialogue—a dialogue that neither preaches nor placates but challenges its participants to work both singly and together in the task of reinterpreting sacred texts. Mike and Rami discuss the nature of divinity, the power of faith, the beauty of myth and story, the necessity of doubt, the achievements, failings, and future of religion, and, above all, the struggle to live ethically and in harmony with the way of God.   978-1-57312-612-0 144 pages/pb **$15.00**

Mount and Mountain
Vol. 2: A Reverend and a Rabbi Talk About the Sermon on the Mount
Rami Shapiro and Michael Smith

This book, focused on the Sermon on the Mount, represents the second half of Mike and Rami's dialogue. In it, Mike and Rami explore the text of Jesus' sermon cooperatively, contributing perspectives drawn from their lives and religious traditions and seeking moments of illumination.   978-1-57312-654-0 254 pages/pb **$19.00**

Overcoming Adolescence
Growing Beyond Childhood into Maturity
Marion D. Aldridge

In *Overcoming Adolescence*, Marion Aldridge poses questions for adults of all ages to consider. His challenge to readers is one he has personally worked to confront: to grow up *all the way*—mentally, physically, academically, socially, emotionally, and spiritually. The key involves not only knowing how to work through the process but also how to recognize what may be contributing to our perpetual adolescence.

978-1-57312-577-2 156 pages/pb **$17.00**

Psychic Pancakes & Communion Pizza
More Musings and Mutterings of a Church Misfit
Bert Montgomery

Psychic Pancakes & Communion Pizza is Bert Montgomery's highly anticipated follow-up to *Elvis, Willie, Jesus & Me* and contains further reflections on music, film, culture, life, and finding Jesus in the midst of it all.   978-1-57312-578-9 160 pages/pb **$16.00**

To order call **1-800-747-3016** or visit **www.helwys.com**

Quiet Faith
An Introvert's Guide to Spiritual Survival
Judson Edwards

In eight finely crafted chapters, Edwards look at key issues like evangelism, interpreting the Bible, dealing with doubt, and surviving the church from the perspective of a confirmed, but sometimes reluctant, introvert. In the process, he offers some provocative insights that introverts will find helpful and reassuring.

978-1-57312-681-6 144 pages/pb **$15.00**

Reading Ezekiel (Reading the Old Testament series)
A Literary and Theological Commentary
Marvin A. Sweeney

The book of Ezekiel points to the return of YHWH to the holy temple at the center of a reconstituted Israel and creation at large. As such, the book of Ezekiel portrays the purging of Jerusalem, the Temple, and the people, to reconstitute them as part of a new creation at the conclusion of the book. With Jerusalem, the Temple, and the people so purged, YHWH stands once again in the holy center of the created world.

978-1-57312-658-8 264 pages/pb **$22.00**

Reading Job (Reading the Old Testament series)
A Literary and Theological Commentary
James L. Crenshaw

At issue in the Book of Job is a question with which most all of us struggle at some point in life, "Why do bad things happen to good people?" James Crenshaw has devoted his life to studying the disturbing matter of theodicy—divine justice—that troubles many people of faith.

978-1-57312-574-1 192 pages/pb **$22.00**

Reading Judges (Reading the Old Testament series)
A Literary and Theological Commentary
Mark E. Biddle

Reading the Old Testament book of Judges presents a number of significant challenges related to social contexts, historical settings, and literary characteristics. Acknowledging and examining these difficulties provides a point of entry into the world of Judges and promises to enrich the reading experience.

978-1-57312-631-1 240 pages/pb **$22.00**

To order call 1-800-747-3016 or visit www.helwys.com

Reading Samuel (Reading the Old Testament series)
A Literary and Theological Commentary
Johanna W. H. van Wijk-Bos

Interpreted masterfully by preeminent Old Testament scholar Johanna W. H. van Wijk-Bos, the story of Samuel touches on a vast array of subjects that make up the rich fabric of human life. The reader gains an inside look at leadership, royal intrigue, military campaigns, occult practices, and the significance of religious objects of veneration.

978-1-57312-607-6 272 pages/pb **$22.00**

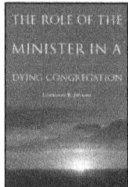

The Role of the Minister in a Dying Congregation
Lynwood B. Jenkins

Jenkins provides a courageous and responsible resource on one of the most critical issues in congregational life: how to help a congregation conclude its ministry life cycle with dignity and meaning.

978-1-57312-571-0 96 pages/pb **$14.00**

Sessions with Genesis (Session Bible Studies series)
The Story Begins
Tony W. Cartledge

Immersing us in the book of Genesis, Tony Cartledge examines both its major stories and the smaller cycles of hope and failure, of promise and judgment. Genesis introduces these themes of divine faithfulness and human failure in unmistakable terms, tracing Israel's beginning to the creation of the world and professing a belief that Israel's particular history had universal significance.

978-1-57312-636-6 144 pages/pb **$14.00**

Sessions with Philippians (Session Bible Studies series)
Finding Joy in Community
Bo Prosser

In this brief letter to the Philippians, Paul makes clear the centrality of his faith in Jesus Christ, his love for the Philippian church, and his joy in serving both Christ and their church.

978-1-57312-579-6 112 pages/pb **$13.00**

Sessions with Samuel (Session Bible Studies series)
Stories from the Edge
Tony W. Cartledge

In these stories, Israel faces one crisis after another, a people constantly on the edge. Individuals such as Saul and David find themselves on the edge as well, facing troubles of leadership and personal struggle. Yet, each crisis becomes a gateway for learning that God is always present, that hope remains.

978-1-57312-555-0 112 pages/pb **$13.00**

To order call 1-800-747-3016 or visit www.helwys.com

Silver Linings
My Life Before and After Challenger 7
June Scobee Rodgers

We know the public story of *Challenger 7*'s tragic destruction. That day, June's life took a new direction that ultimately led to the creation of the Challenger Center and to new life and new love. Her story of Christian faith and triumph over adversity will inspire readers of every age.   978-1-57312-570-3 352 pages/hc **$28.00**

Spacious
Exploring Faith and Place
Holly Sprink

Exploring where we are and why that matters to God is an ongoing process. If we are present and attentive, God creatively and continuously widens our view of the world, whether we live in the Amazon or in our own hometown.   978-1-57312-649-6 156 pages/pb **$16.00**

This Is What a Preacher Looks Like
Sermons by Baptist Women in Ministry
Pamela Durso, ed.

In this collection of sermons by thirty-six Baptist women, their voices are soft and loud, prophetic and pastoral, humorous and sincere. They are African American, Asian, Latina, and Caucasian. They are sisters, wives, mothers, grandmothers, aunts, and friends.
978-1-57312-554-3 144 pages/pb **$18.00**

Transformational Leadership
Leading with Integrity
Charles B. Bugg

"Transformational" leadership involves understanding and growing so that we can help create positive change in the world. This book encourages leaders to be willing to change if *they* want to help transform the world. They are honest about their personal strengths and weaknesses, and are not afraid of doing a fearless moral inventory of themselves.
978-1-57312-558-1 112 pages/pb **$14.00**

To order call **1-800-747-3016** or visit **www.helwys.com**

Clarence Jordan's
Cotton Patch Gospel

The Complete Collection

Hardback • 448 pages
Retail 50.00 • Your Price 45.00

The Cotton Patch Gospel, by Koinonia Farm founder Clarence Jordan, recasts the stories of Jesus and the letters of the New Testament into the language and culture of the mid-twentieth-century South. Born out of the civil rights struggle, these now-classic translations of much of the New Testament bring the far-away places of Scripture closer to home: Gainesville, Selma, Birmingham, Atlanta, Washington D.C.

More than a translation, *The Cotton Patch Gospel* continues to make clear the startling relevance of Scripture for today. Now for the first time collected in a single, hardcover volume, this edition comes complete with a new Introduction by President Jimmy Carter, a Foreword by Will D. Campbell, and an Afterword by Tony Campolo. Smyth & Helwys Publishing is proud to help reintroduce these seminal works of Clarence Jordan to a new generation of believers, in an edition that can be passed down to generations still to come.

 To order call **1-800-747-3016**
or visit **www.helwys.com**

www.ingramcontent.com/pod-product-compliance
Lightning Source LLC
Chambersburg PA
CBHW071702040426
42446CB00011B/1879